Count us in!
A Pack to Support the Numeracy Hour
Key Stages 1 & 2

The Questions Publishing Company & Staffordshire County Council, 1999

First Published 1999

This edition published by
The Questions Publishing Company Ltd
27 Frederick Street, Birmingham B1 3HH

This edition designed by Stuart Clarke
Illustrations by Janet Thorne
Cover design by Steven Molloy

Original design by
SENSS Enterprises
Special Educational Needs Support Service
Flash Ley Resource Centre
Hawksmoor Road
STAFFORD
ST17 9DR

Tel: 01785-356853
Fax: 01785-356854

Contents

Acknowledgements

Compiled by:
Staffordshire Special Educational Needs Support Service
Numeracy Co-ordinators

Ruth Rowley
Sandra Garner
Marjorie Thorley
Alison Forrest
Hilary Standen
Jill Higginson

Number Rhymes and Jingles for Young Children

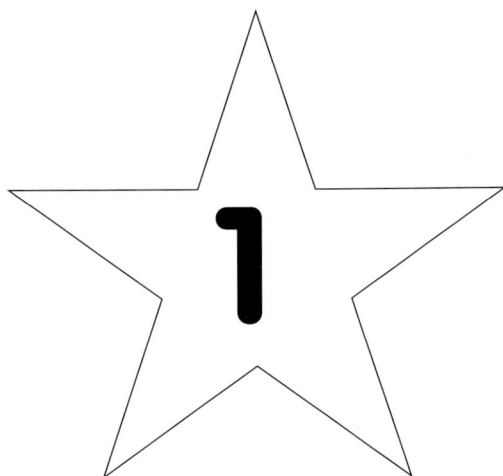

1

2

3

4

5

Contents

Incey Wincey Spider
Climbed up the spout.
Down came the raindrops,
And washed poor Wincey out.
Out came the sunshine,
And dried up all the rain,
And Incey Wincey Spider
Climbed up the spout again.

Hickory, dickory, dock,
The mouse ran up the clock.
The clock struck one,
The mouse run down,
Hickory, dickory, dock.

Here we go, up, up, up,
Here we go, down, down, down,
Here we go backwards and forwards,
Here we go round and round.

This little piggy went to market,
This little piggy stayed at home,
This little piggy had roast beef,
This little piggy had none,
This little piggy cried "eeee" all the way home.

Round and round the haystack,
Ran the little mouse,
One step, two steps,
Into his little house.

Two little dicky birds,

Sitting on a wall,

One called Peter,

One called Paul.

Fly away Peter,

Fly away Paul,

Come back Peter,

Come back Paul.

Baa baa black sheep,

Have you any wool?

Yes sir, yes sir,

Three bags full;

One for the master,

And one for the dame,

And one for the little boy

Who lives down the lane.

Two little hands go clap, clap, clap,
Two little arms lie in my lap,
Two little feet go bump, bump, bump,
Two little legs give a great big jump.

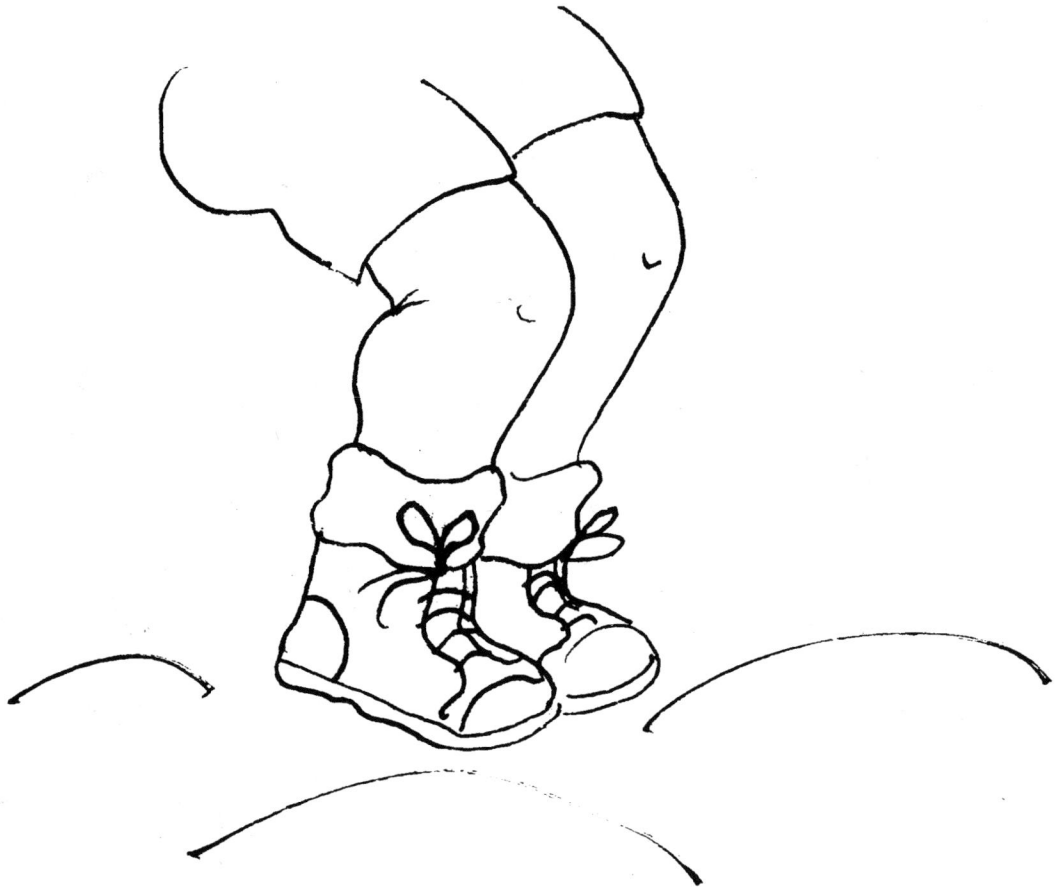

Two fat gentlemen met in the lane,
Bowed most politely, bowed once again.
How do you do?
And how do you do?
And how do you do again.

Two tall ladies,
(First fingers)
Two big policemen,
(Middle fingers)
Two thin schoolboys,
(Ring fingers)
Two little babies,
(Little fingers).

One is fairly light and neat,
Two is a giant who stamps his feet,
Three is a mouse who crouches small,
Four is a great big bouncing ball.

Five little birds without any homes,
Five little trees in a row,
Come build your nest in our branches tall,
And we'll rock you to and fro.

Ten little gentlemen standing in a row,
Bow little gentlemen,
Bow down low.
Walk little gentlemen right across the floor.
Please little gentlemen shut the door.

Ten little fingers,

Ten little toes,

Two little ears,

And one little nose.

Two little eyes

That shine so bright,

And one little mouth

To kiss goodnight.

1

2

3

4

5

One, two,
What shall I do?

Three, four,
Play on the floor.

Five, six,
Build with bricks.

Seven, eight,
Make a gate.

Nine, ten,
Knock it down again.

10

9

8

7

6

Ruth Ainsworth

A Counting Rhyme

One little,

Two little,

Three little pigs,

Small and fat and pink,

Fell into a tub of tar,

And turned as black as ink.

Four little,

Five little,

Six little pigs,

Went to the moon.

They found it colder than they thought,

And came back very soon.

Seven little,

Eight little,

Nine little pigs,

Went to look for gold:

They found it in a pickle-jar,

At least, that's what I'm told.

M.M. Stephenson

Black Monkeys

One black monkey swinging in a tree,
Two black monkeys paddling in the sea.

Three black monkeys playing on a swing,
Four black monkeys dancing in a ring.

Five black monkeys drinking lemonade,
Six black monkeys digging with a spade.

Seven black monkeys wearing sailor hats,
Eight black monkeys waving cricket bats.

Nine black monkeys standing on their heads,
Ten black monkeys sleeping in their beds.

Magpies

One for sorrow,
Two for joy,
Three for a girl,
Four for a boy,
Five for silver,
Six for gold,
Seven for a secret,
That's never been told.

Cherry song

One, two, three, four,
Mary at the cottage door,
Five, six, seven, eight,
Eating cherries off a plate.

3

1

5

2

6

4

Potatoes

One potato, two potato,
Three potato, four,
Five potato, six potato,
Seven potato, more!

One, Two, Three, Four, Five

"One, two, three, four, five,
Once I caught a fish alive,
Six, seven, eight, nine, ten,
Then I let it go again."
"Why did you let it go?"
"Because it bit my finger so."
"Which finger did it bite?"
"This little finger on the right."

Nick-Nack Paddy-Wack

This old man he played one,
He played nick-nack on my gun.
With a nick-nack paddy-wack,
Give a dog a bone,
This old man came rolling home.

etc.

two – shoe

three – knee

four – door

five – hive

six – sticks

seven – going to Devon

eight – gate

nine – line

ten – hen

One, two, buckle my shoe

One, two, buckle my shoe;
Three, four, knock at the door;
Five, six, pick up sticks;
Seven, eight, lay them straight;
Nine, ten, a good fat hen.
Eleven, twelve, dig and delve;
Thirteen, fourteen, maids a-courting;
Fifteen, sixteen, maids in the kitchen;
Seventeen, eighteen, maids a-waiting;
Nineteen, twenty, my plate's empty.

When I was one

When I was one,
I was just begun.

When I was two,
I was nearly new.

When I was three,
I was hardly me.

When I was four,
I was not much more.

When I was five,
I was just alive.

But now I'm six,
I'm as clever, as clever,
So I think I'll be six,
For ever and ever.

One elephant

1 elephant went out to play,
Upon a spider's web one day,
He found it such enormous fun,
That he called for another elephant to come.

2 elephants went out to play etc.

One man went to mow

One man went to mow,
Went to mow a meadow,
One man and his dog,
Went to mow a meadow.

Two men went etc.

Five currant buns

5 currant buns in a baker's shop,
Big and round with sugar on the top,
Along came .... with a penny one day,
Bought a currant bun and took it away.

4 currant buns etc.

Five little ducks

Five little ducks went swimming one day,
Over the hills and far away,
Mother duck cried, "Quack, quack, quack, quack,"
But only four little ducks came back.

Four little ducks etc.

Last verse:

One little duck went swimming one day,
Over the hills and far away,
Mother duck cried, "Quack, quack, quack, quack,"
And five little ducks came swimming back.

Little Dicky Birds

One little dicky bird,
Hopped on my shoe;
Along came another one,
And that made two.

Chorus: Fly to the tree tops;
Fly to the ground;
Fly, little dicky birds,
Round and round.

Two little dicky birds,
Singing in a tree;
Along came another one,
And that made three. (Chorus)

Three little dicky birds,
Came to my door;
Along came another one,
And that made four. (Chorus)

Four little dicky birds,
Perched on a hive;
Along came another one,
And that made five. (Chorus)

Five little dicky birds,
Nesting in the ricks;
Along came another one,
And that made six. (Chorus)

Six little dicky birds,
Flying up to heaven;
Along came another one,
And that made seven. (Chorus)

Seven little dicky birds,
Sat upon a gate;
Along came another one,
And that made eight. (Chorus)

Eight little dicky birds,
Swinging on a line;
Along came another one,
And that made nine. (Chorus)

Nine little dicky birds,
Looking at a hen;
Along came another one,
And that made ten. (Chorus)

10 in a bed

There were 10 in a bed and the little one said,
"Roll over, roll over."
So they all rolled over and one fell out:
There were 9 in a bed and the little one said... etc.

10 green bottles

10 green bottles
Hanging on the wall,
10 green bottles
Hanging on the wall,
But if one green bottle
Should accidentally fall,
There'd be 9 green bottles
Hanging on the wall.
etc.

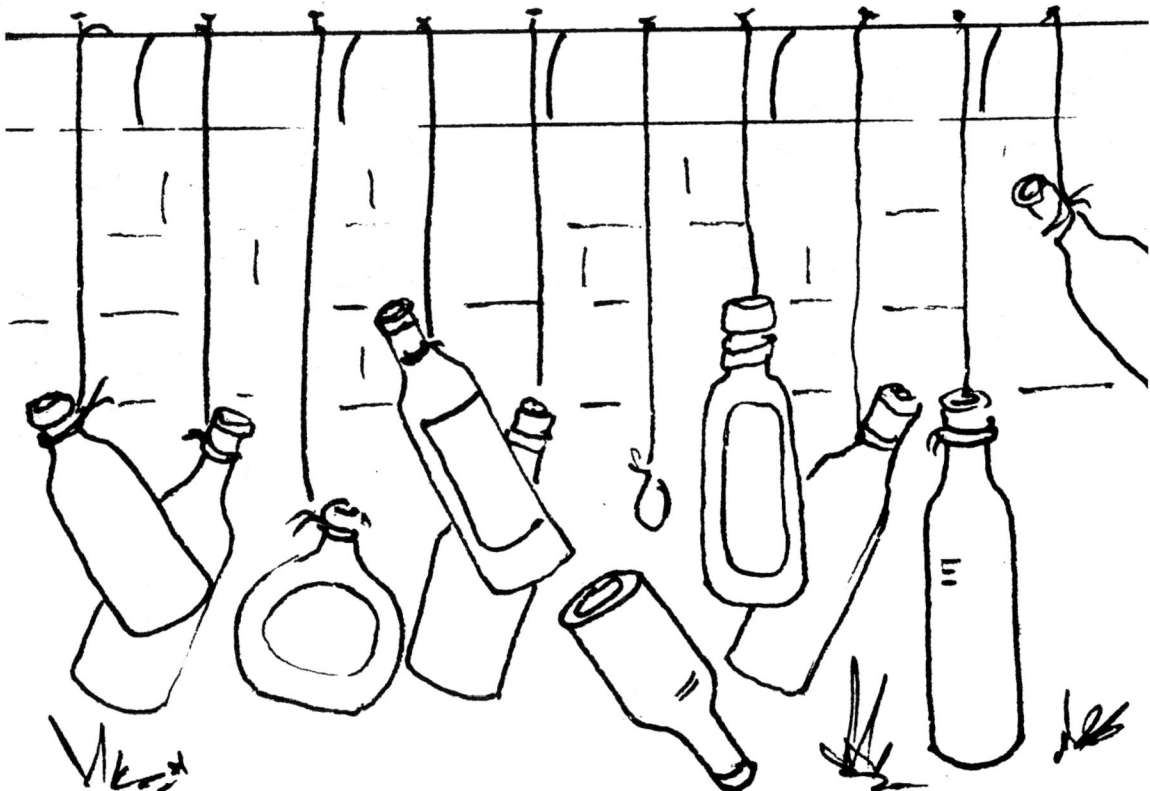

Time

Hours of the day.
Game: 'What's the time, Mr. Wolf?'

Seasons

Spring is flowery, showery, bowery,
Summer is hoppy, croppy, poppy,
Autumn is slippy, drippy, nippy,
Winter is wheezy, sneezy, freezy.

Days of the month

Thirty days hath September,
April, June and November.
All the rest have thirty-one,
But February's a different one.
It has twenty-eight days clear,
and twenty-nine each leap year.

Number Cards

1

2

3

4

5

6

7

8

9

10

11

12

13

14

15

16

17

18

19

20

21

22

23

24

25

26

27

28

29

30

31

32

33

34

35

36

37

38

39

40

41

42

43

44

45

46

47

48

49

50

51

52

53

54

55

56

57

58

59

60

61

62

63

64

65

66

67

68

69

70

71

72

73

74

75

76

77

78

79

80

81

82

83

84

85

86

87

88

89

90

91

92

93

94

95

96

97

98

99

100

Days of the Week

Sunday

Monday

Tuesday

Wednesday

Thursday

Friday

Saturday

Months of the Year

January

February

March

April

May

June

July

August

September

October

November

December

Animal Pairs

A Matching Game

Animal Pairs

A matching game for 2 or more players.

Aim

To develop matching and visual discrimination skills.

Instructions

1. Photocopy 2 sets of pictures onto card.

2. Colour each animal to make matching pairs. Cut out and laminate.

3. Place all the cards face down on the table.

4. First player picks up 2 cards.

5. If the cards are the same, the player wins the pair and has another turn.

6. If the cards do not match, the cards are replaced face down on the table and play passes to the next player.

7. The winner is the player with the most pairs at the end of the game.

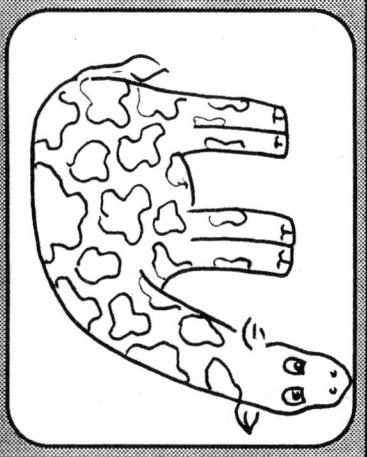

Red, Blue, Red, Blue, Red, Blue ...

Pattern Completion & Sequencing

Pattern Completion and Sequencing

Pattern completion and sequencing are essential prerequisites for developing algebraic concepts. In Early Years and KS1, children are introduced to pattern, ordering and visual representations as foundations to developing abstract concepts.

Instructions

Use the masters to produce a variety of baseboards.

1. Copy masters onto card.

2. Colour the first two, three and four shapes so that the child has a colour pattern to follow.

3. Laminate the baseboards.

Alternatively photocopy for colouring-in sheets.

How to Play

The child continues the colour sequences by colouring, or placing counters on the board to continue the sequence.

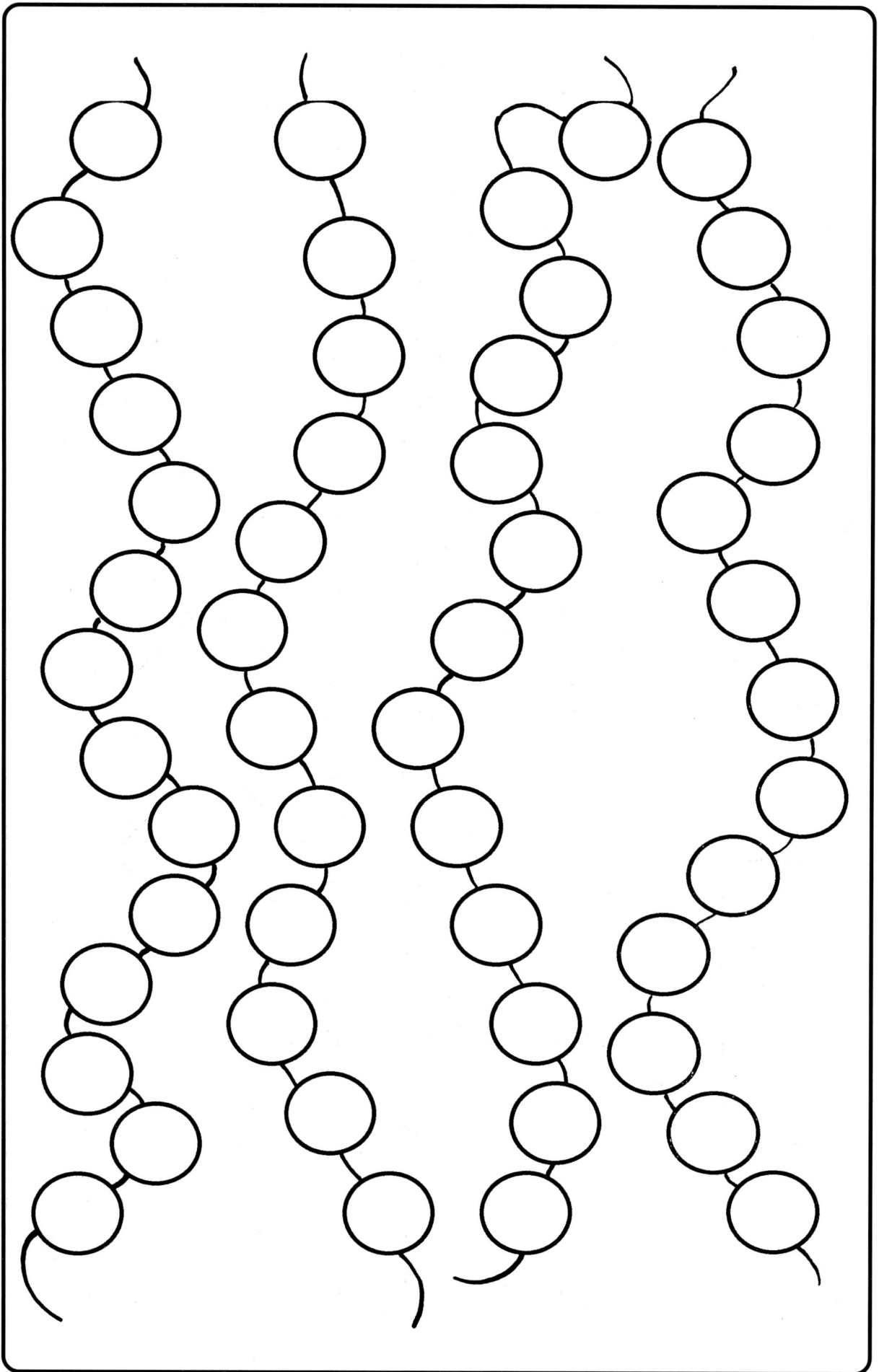

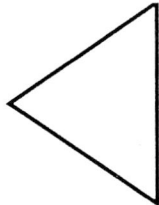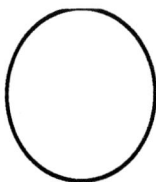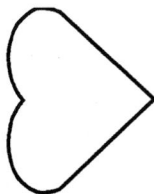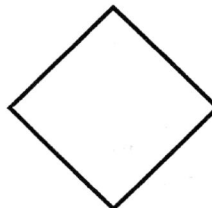
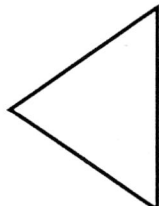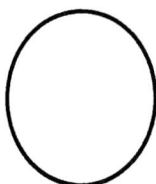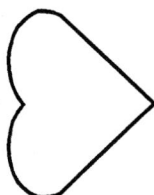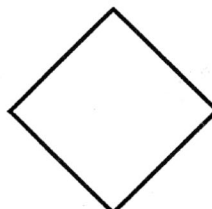
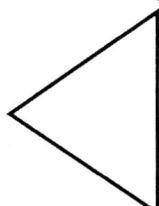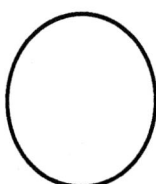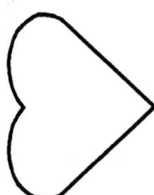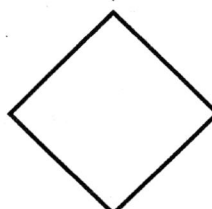
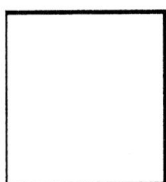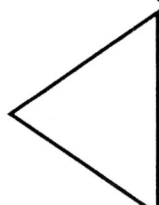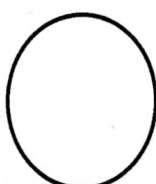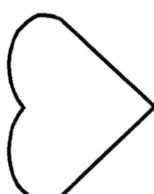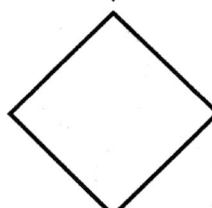
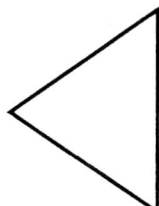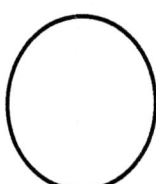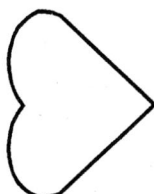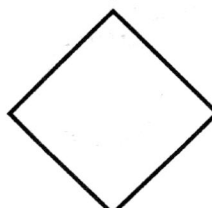
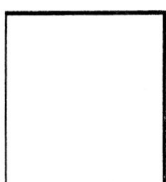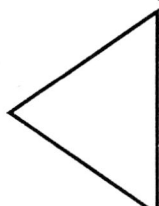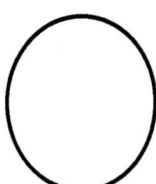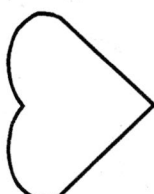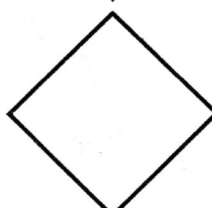
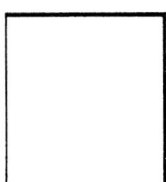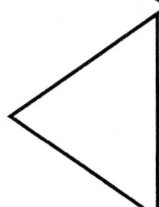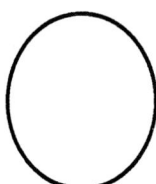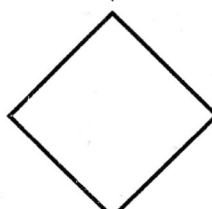
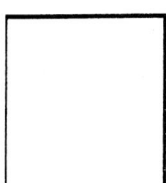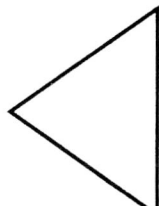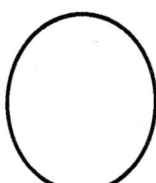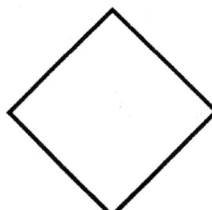

Build a Ted

Matching and counting

Build a Ted
Matching and number recognition

Instructions

1. Photocopy 8 'Teds' onto card.

2. Cut 4 'Teds' into individual pieces.

3. Laminate the other 4 'Teds' as baseboards.

Equipment needed

One die

How to Play

Children take it in turns to throw the die and pick up a corresponding piece from the pile in the centre of the table.

A body (6) will need to be gained before any other piece.
The head (5) will need to be gained before the ears.
The first child to build a complete Ted is the winner.

Build a Ted

Teddy Bear's Picnic

Matching and counting

Teddy Bear's Picnic
Matching and number recognition

Instructions

1. Photocopy 4 copies of each sheet.

2. Cut out pieces:

2. Cut out pieces: Plate 6 or ⠿   Cake 3 or ⠆

                        Teapot 5 or ⠣   Jelly 2 or ⠁

                        Cup 4 or ⠒   Spoon 1 or •

Equipment needed

One die

How to Play

Children take it in turns to throw the die and pick up a corresponding piece from the pile in the centre of the table.

A plate (6) will need to be gained before a cake.
The first child to collect all the pieces for their picnic, is the winner.

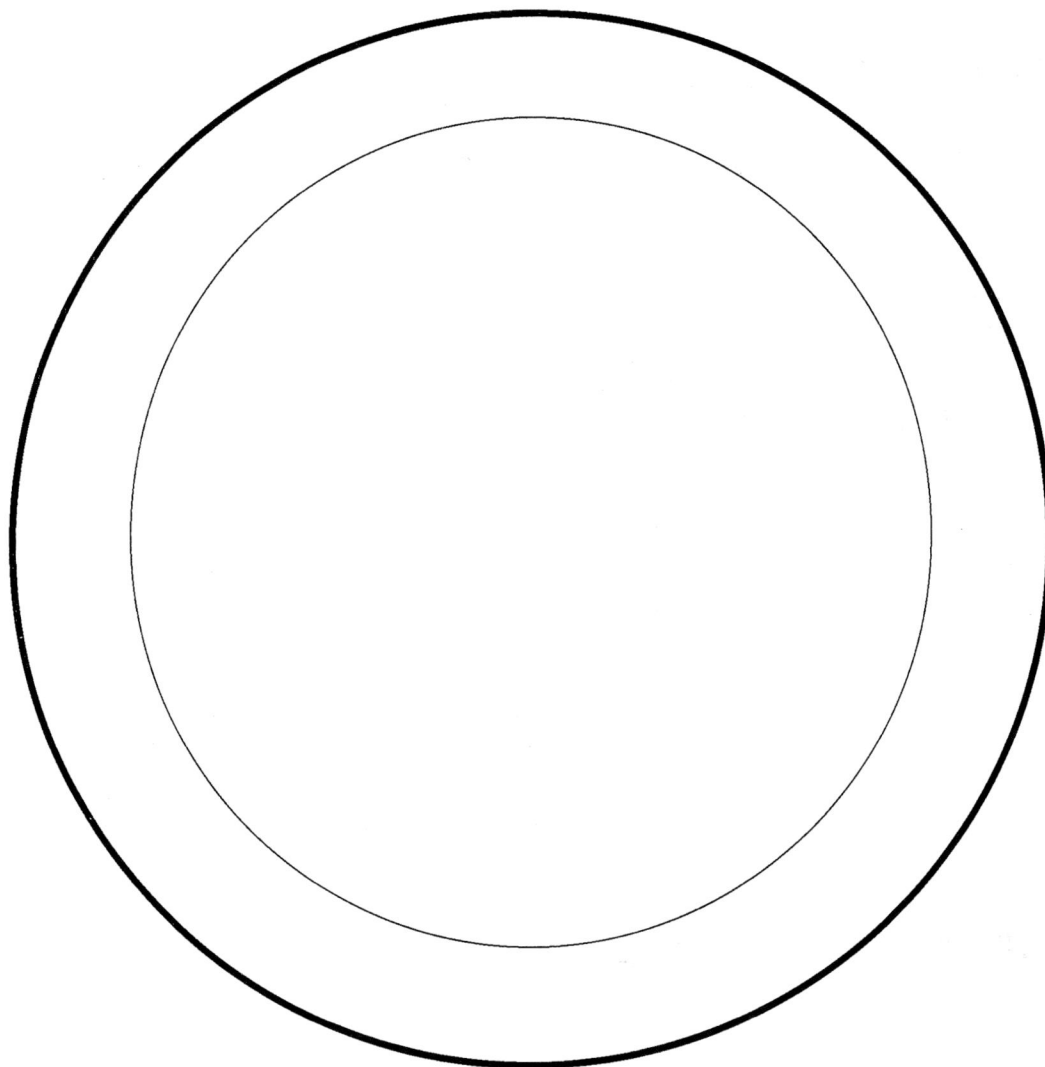

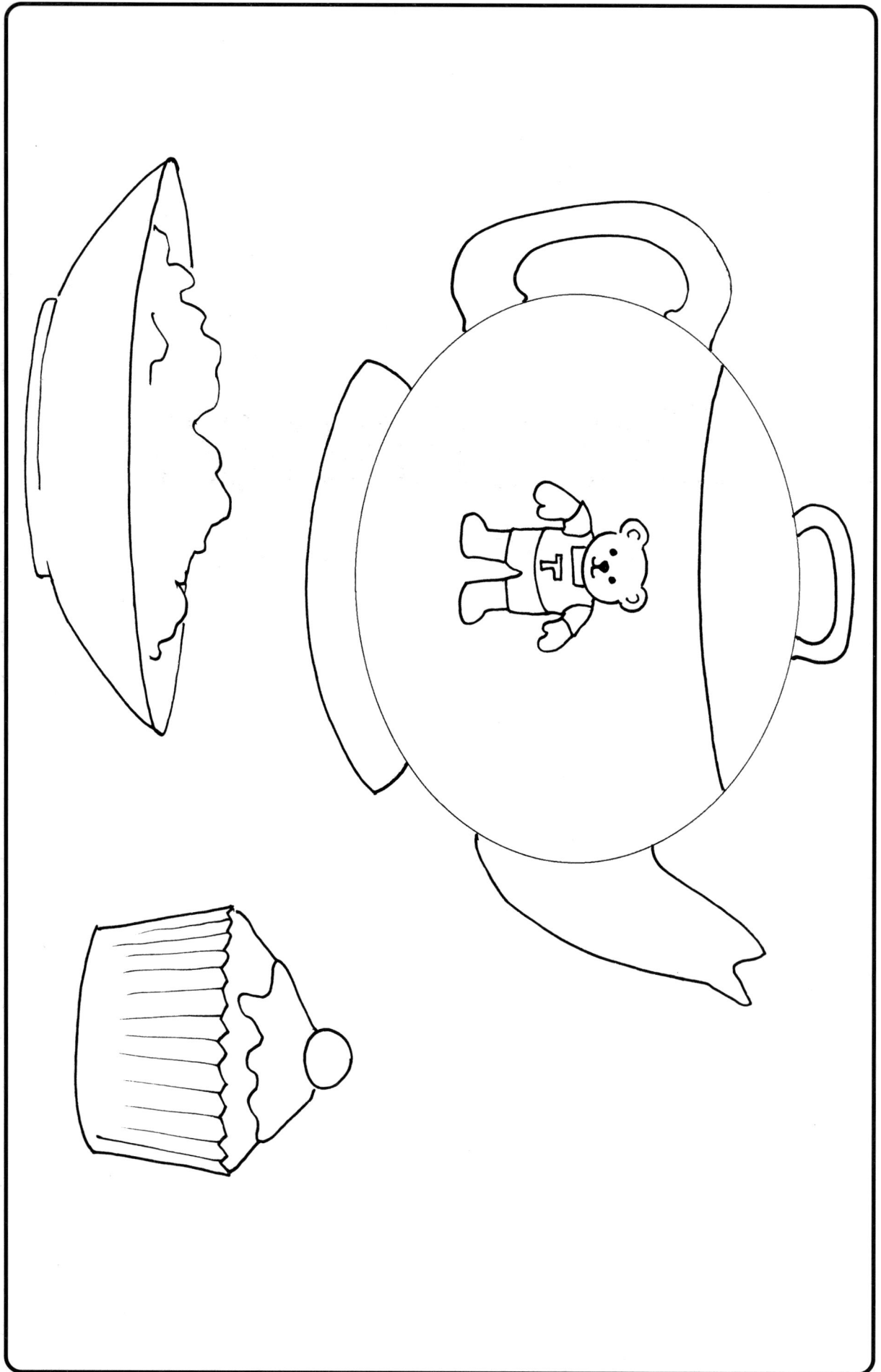

Dominoes
Matching and counting

Dominoes

Instructions

1. Photocopy the masters onto card.

2. Cut out the individual pieces.

3. Colour and laminate.

How to Play

Dominoes can be used with a small group playing competitively or by individuals as a self-checking game.

Apart from standard dominoes, it is possible to make many different sets.

Dominoes with large dots.
Dominoes using limited numbers (eg: 1,2,3).
Dot/digit/word/dominoes.
Shape/colour dominoes.
Money dominoes.
Use Christmas cards to make picture/digit dominoes.

3

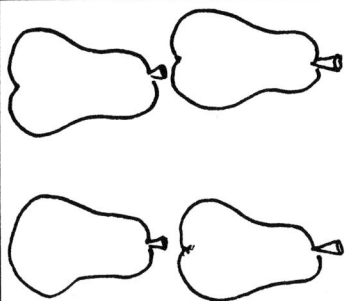

2

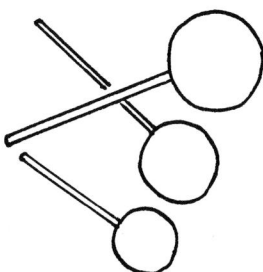

1

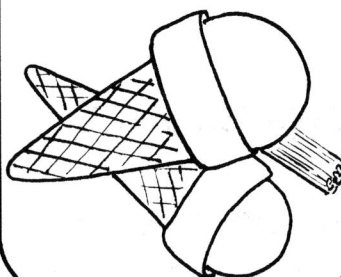

6

5

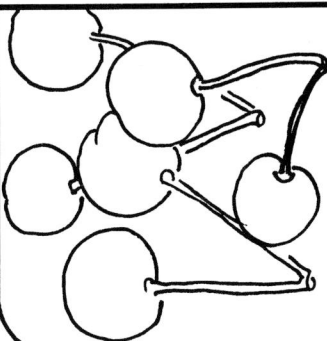

4

9

6

8

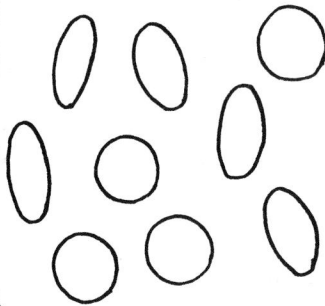

7

10

1		6	
2		7	
3		8	
4		9	
5		10	

Ten Little Soldiers

A Counting Line

Number Bonds to 10

Ten Little Soldiers
Counting and Number Bonds to 10

Instructions

1. Photocopy sheets 1 and 2 onto card.

2. Cut round and cut out the shaded sections.

3. Draw round sheets 1 and 2 onto a larger sheet of card to make one piece with 10 sections. This is the back section.

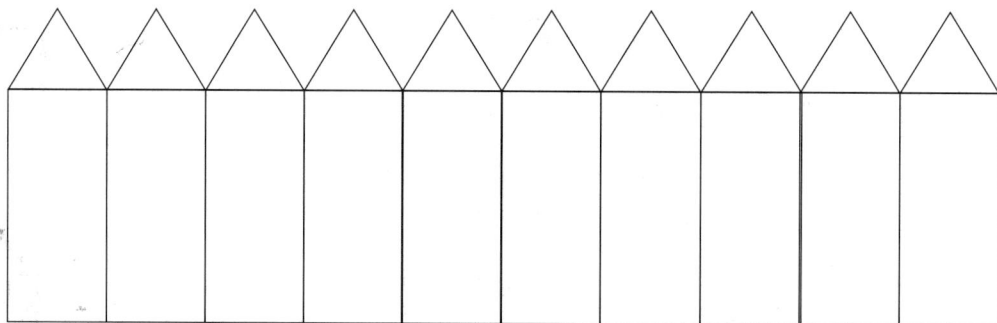

4. Cut out the back section.

5. Photocopy 2 sheets of 'soldiers'.

6. Colour the 'soldiers' and cut out.

7. Insert the 10 'soldiers' between the back section and the two front sections.

8. Glue together, leaving the 'soldiers' standing free.

Use for counting activities, addition and subtraction to 10, number bonds to 10.

		5
		4
		3
		2
		1

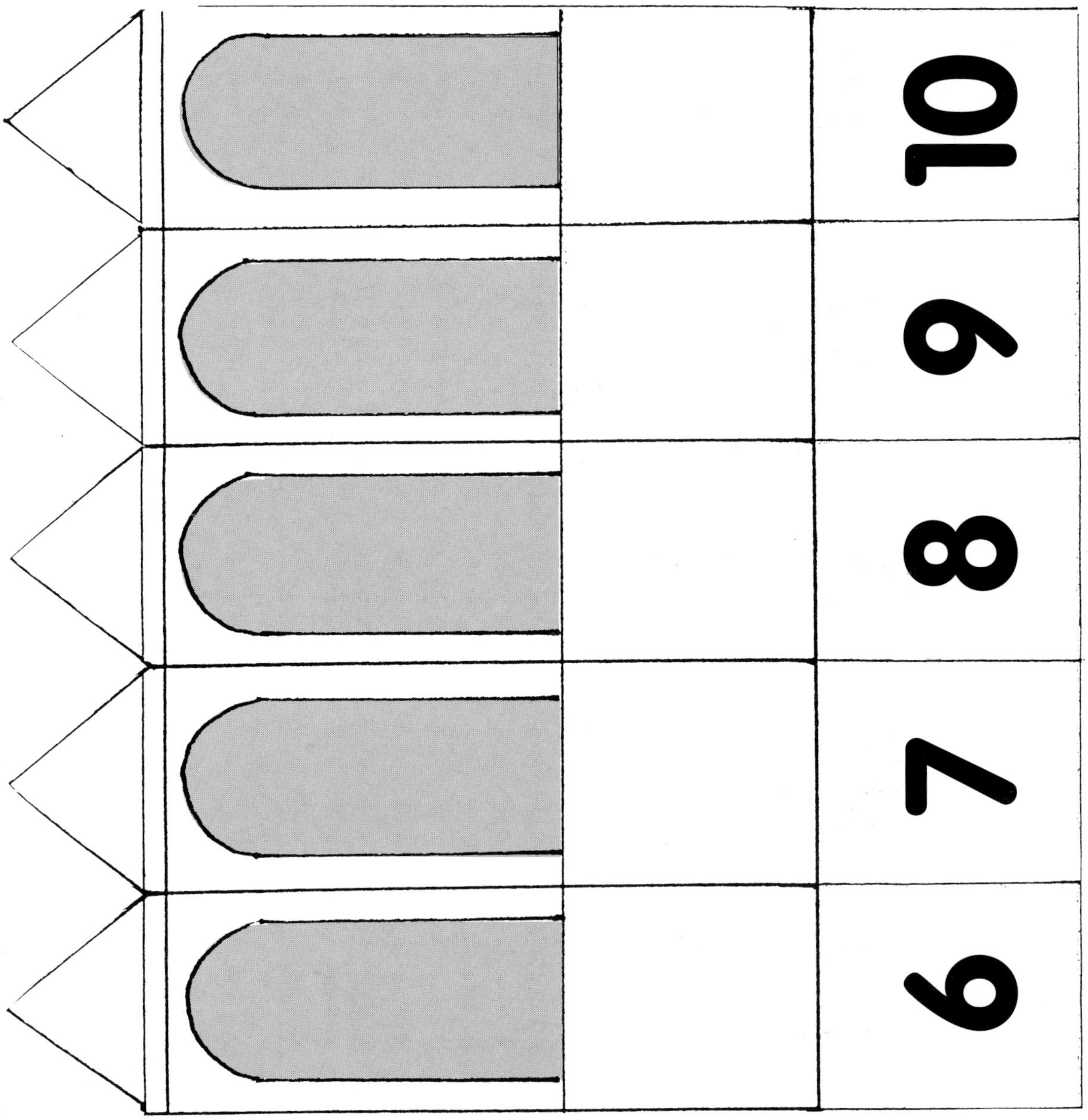
6
7
8
9
10

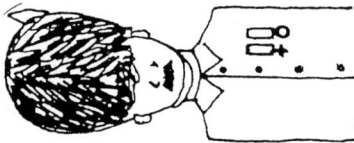
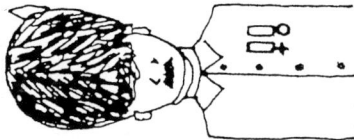
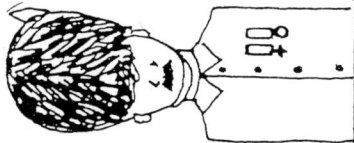
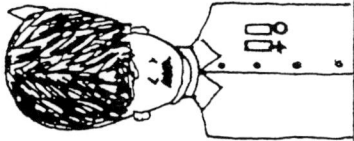

Washing Line Activities

Washing Line Activities

Instructions

1. Photocopy and enlarge number sheets onto card.

2. Cut out and stick on pictures for number in set, e.g. 3 cats / 6 sheep

Equipment needed

1. A line at child height across the classroom.

2. A supply of pegs.

3. Sets of cards for each chosen topic.

Examples of Activities

1. Children to replace cards which have been removed by the teacher.

2. Children to fetch one or more cards as instructed:

> e.g. Fetch no. 3 / all the even numbers/
> a card 2 more than/ less than 8

3. Children to hang a complete set of cards.

4. Children to turn cards to show a number, a pattern or a sequence e.g. a number between 5 and 7, odd numbers.

(See over for some other ideas using sets of cards.)

Washing Line Activities

Use double-sided cards – number in one colour on one side and the same number in a different colour on the other side.

Selected sequences of numbers as appropriate e.g. 1-10, 21-40, even numbers etc.

Days of the Week

Months of the Year

Times of Day – analogue, digital, sequence of daily events (sleeping, getting up, start of school, playtime etc.)

Words e.g. morning, afternoon, evening
            measurement: mm, cm, m, km

Busy Bees

Counting & ordering

Numbers to 10

Busy Bees – A game for 2 players

Instructions

1. Photocopy and enlarge the baseboard to A3.

2. Colour in the baseboard and laminate.

Equipment needed

A coloured counter for each player.

A die with numerals 0, 1, 2 & 3 on four sides and an additional 1 & 2 on the remaining two sides.

Various numbered dice may be used.

How to play

The player rolls the die to decide who starts play. The player with the highest score begins and places his/her counter on the bee. Then she/he rolls the die and moves the number of flowers shown on the face of the die. The next player follows suit. They continue throwing the die until one player reaches the hive. This player is the winner.

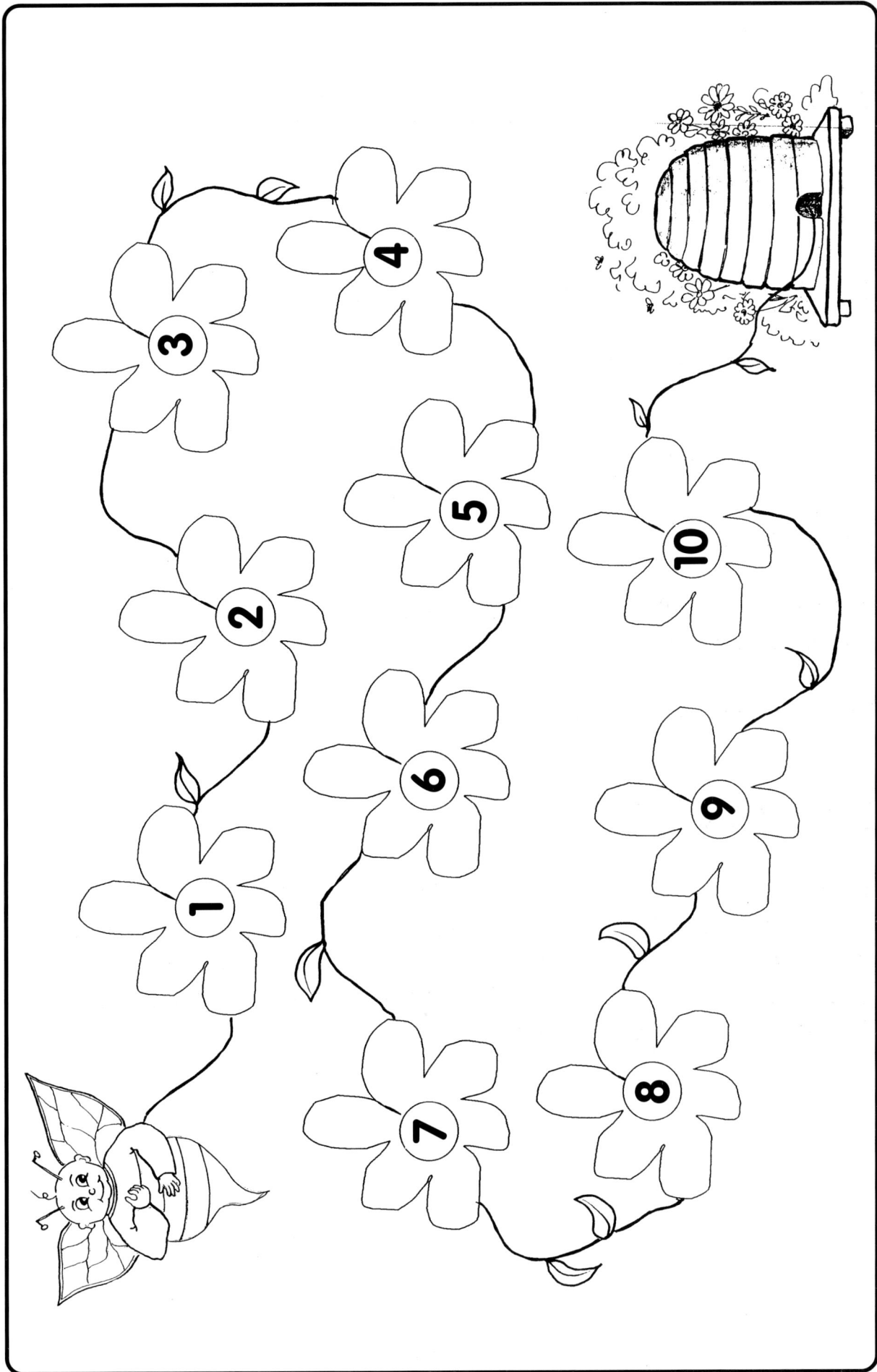

Climb the Stairs

Number Ordering

0-10

0-20

Climb the Stairs

Instructions

1. Photocopy and enlarge the 2 baseboards.

2. Cut off the number section.

3. Colour in the baseboards and laminate.

4. Cut up the numbers and laminate.

You may wish to photocopy the baseboards as individual worksheets.

How to use

Position some of the number cards on the stairs and ask the child to fill in the missing numbers.

Climb the Stairs

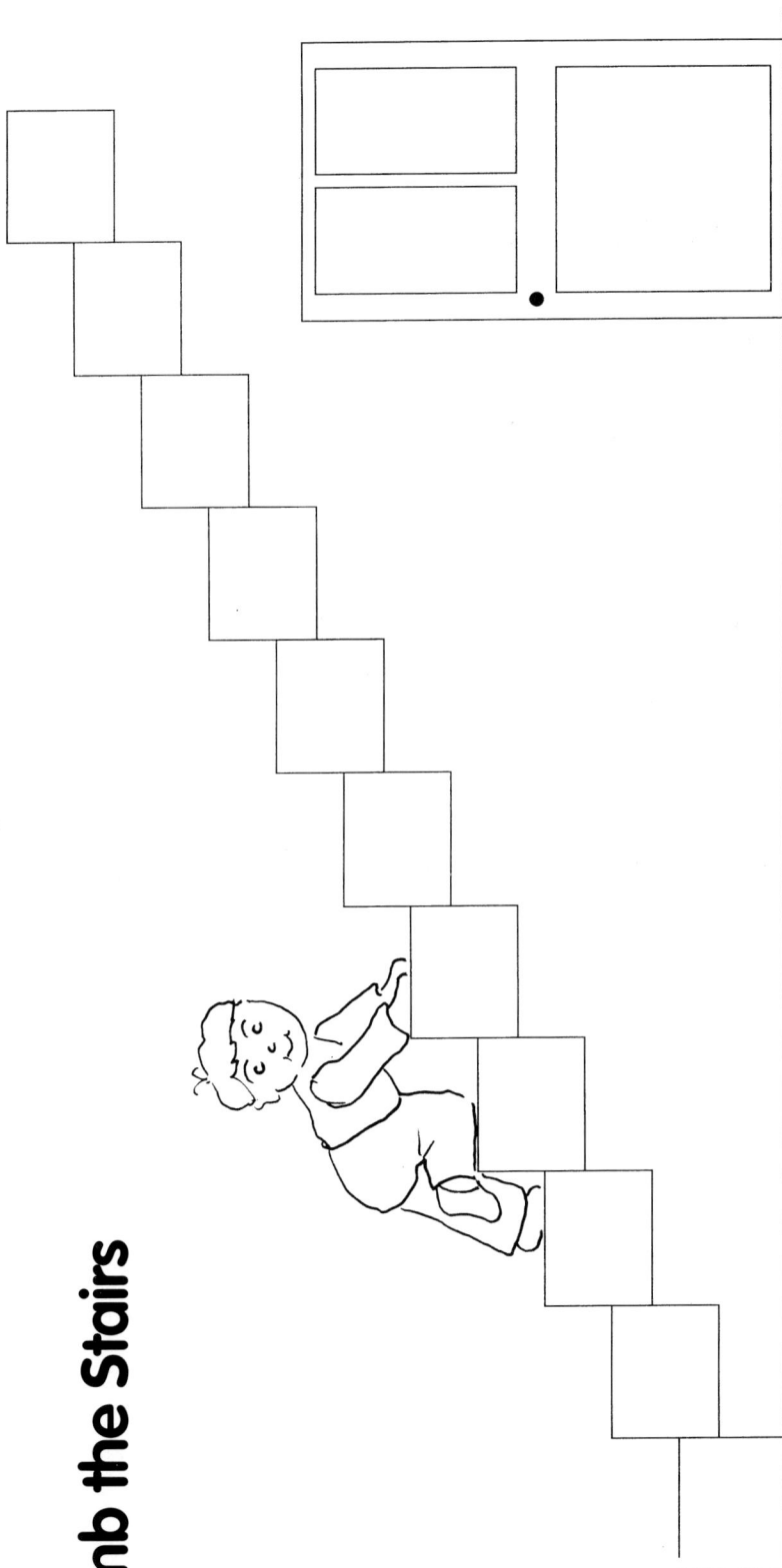

0	1	2	3	4	5	6	7	8	9	10

Climb the Stairs

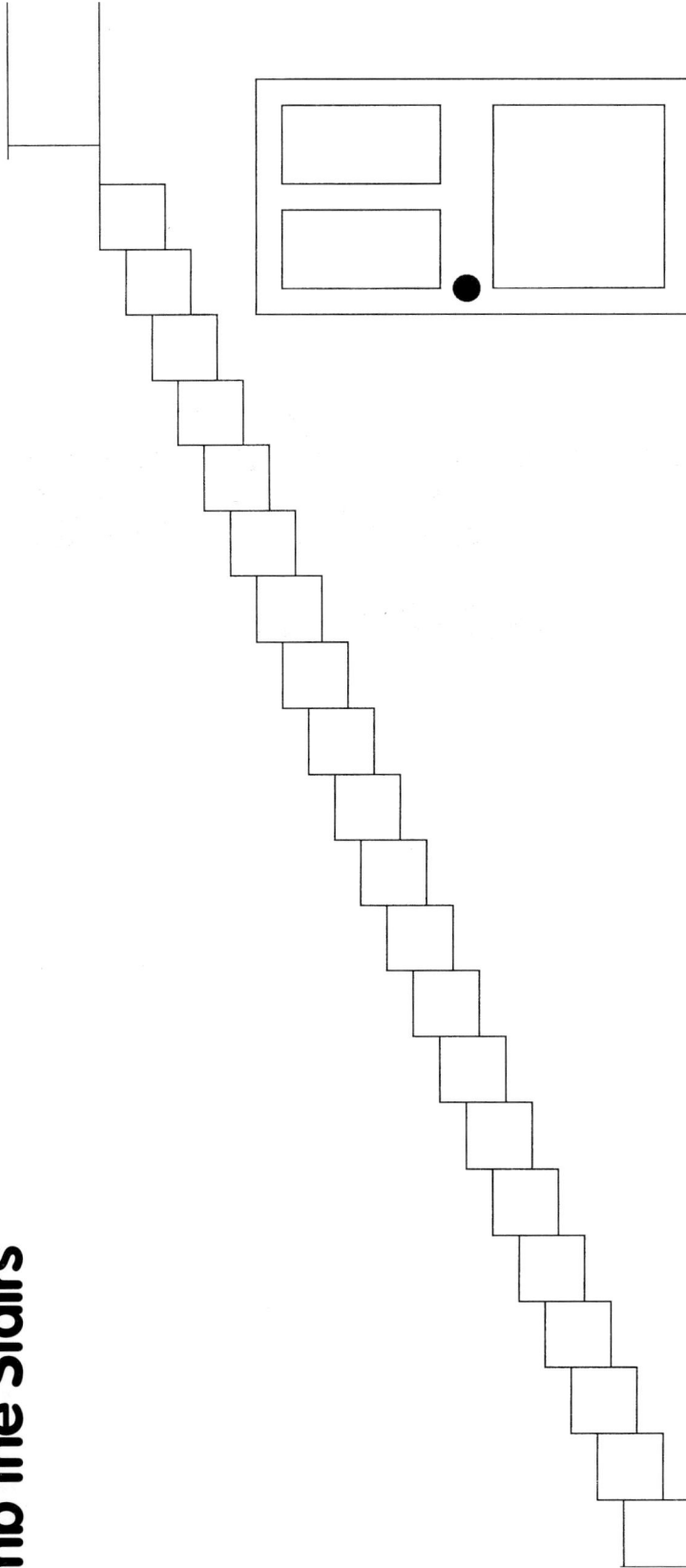

| 0 | 1 | 2 | 3 | 4 | 5 | 6 | 7 | 8 | 9 | 10 |

| 11 | 12 | 13 | 14 | 15 | 16 | 17 | 18 | 19 | 20 |

Bendables

Number Bonds to 10

Bendables

To practise number bonds to 10 (100)

Instructions

1. Photocopy the master sheet.

2. Cut out the squares.

3. Arrange as follows:

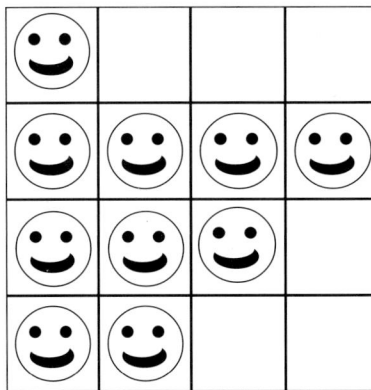

4. Join the squares together with clear sticky tape, leaving gaps so that the squares can be folded along any vertical or horizontal line.

For clowns/1p coins:

● Fold along any vertical or horizontal line to produce each of the numbers 1-10

● Fold as above but state the number pair; e.g. There are 10 clowns, I fold back 3, 7 remain. I can see 5 clowns, 5 are hiding. 5 and 5 make 10 (or 5 plus 5 equals 10)

● Use to find the answer to equations: $3 + \boxed{} = 10$

● For 10p coins use similar activities to demonstrate number bonds to £1.00

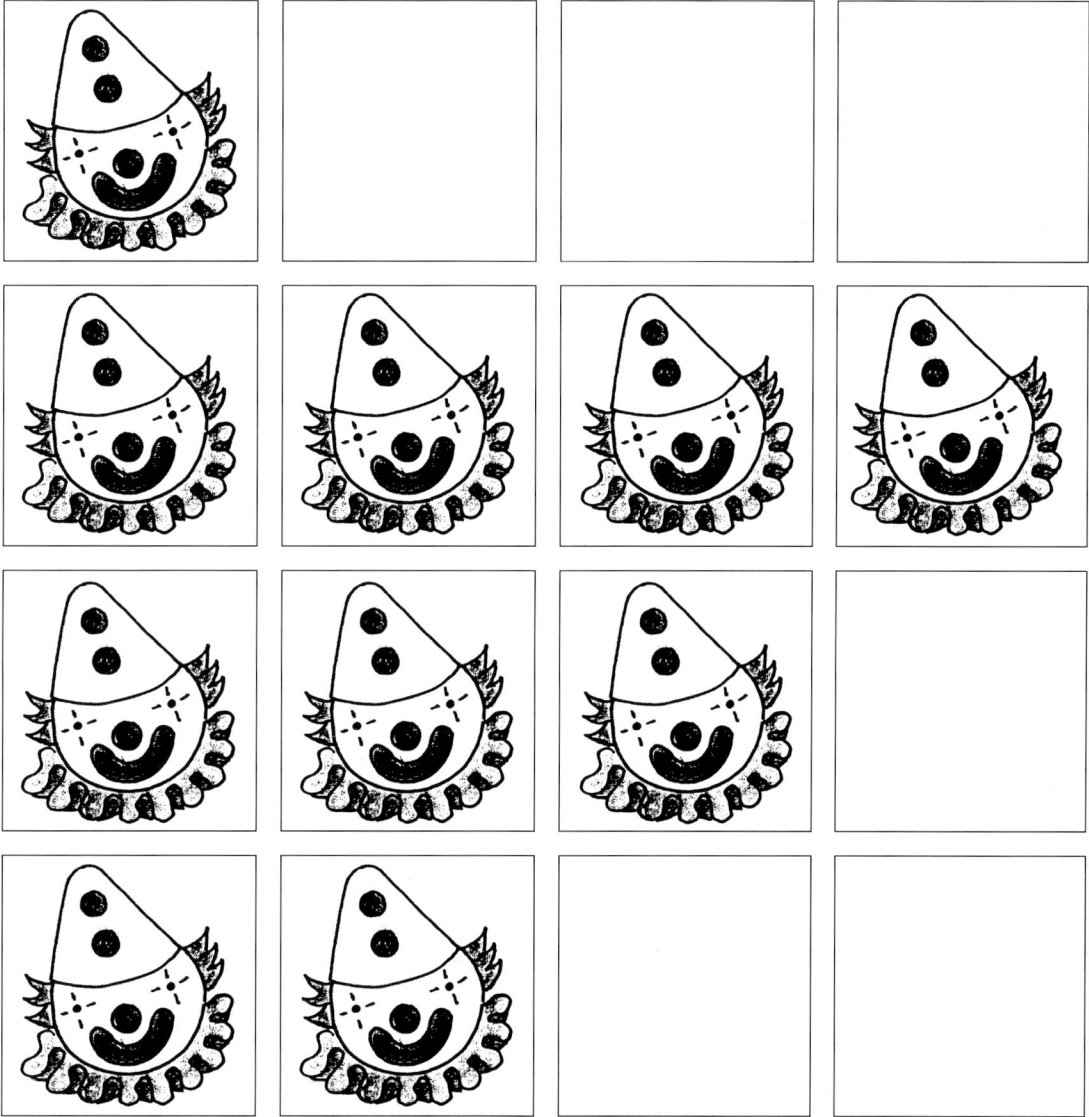

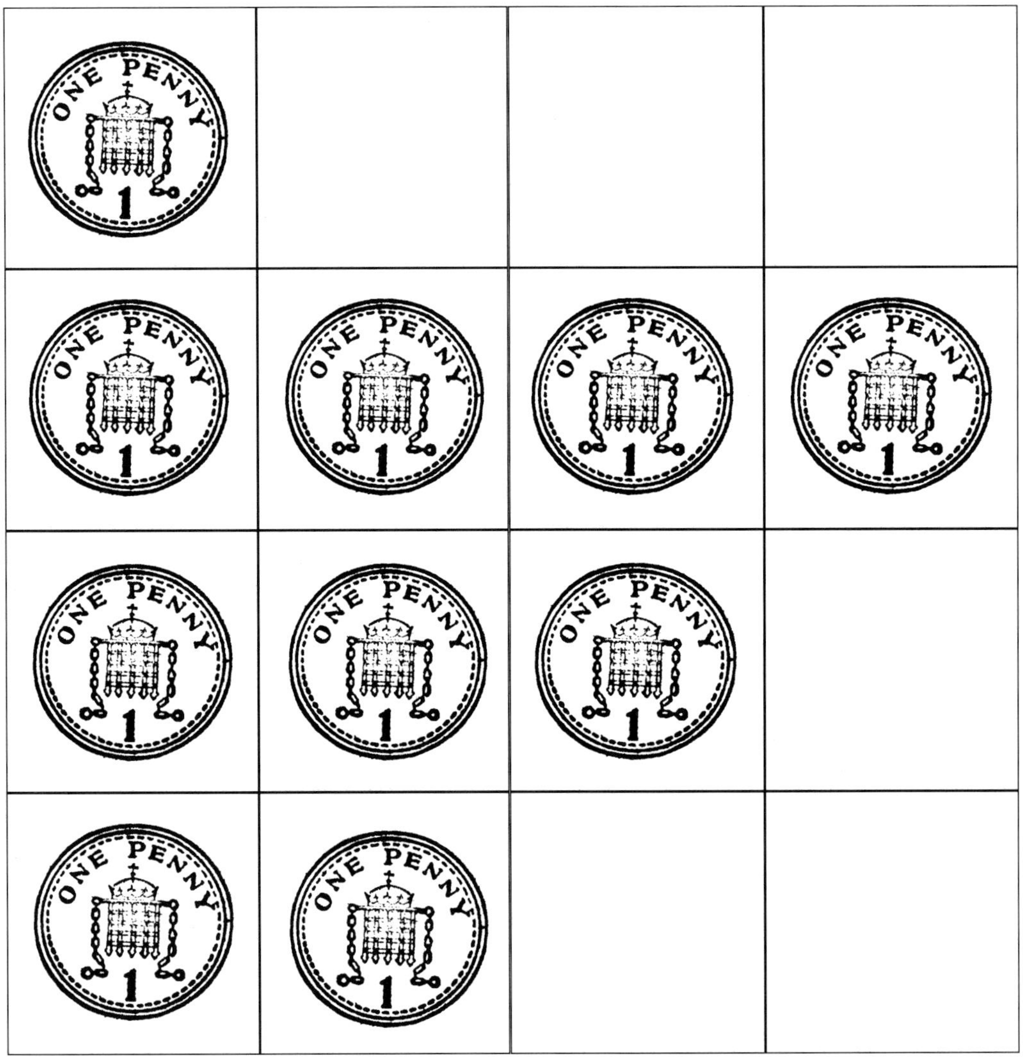
ONE PENNY
1

Shark Chase

Shark Chase

A game for 2 players

Instructions

1. Photocopy and enlarge the baseboard to A3 and stick onto card.

2. Colour and laminate.

Equipment needed

A die (0-5 or 1-6)
Two coloured counters to represent the 'shark' and the 'fish'.

How to play

The children determine who will be the 'shark' and who will be the 'fish', then place their counters on START. The 'fish' throws first, doubles the number shown on the die and moves that number of spaces.
The 'shark' then throws the die, but moves only the actual number of spaces indicated by the die.
The aim is for the 'fish' to get home without being caught by the 'shark'. The fish is deemed caught, if the 'shark' lands on or beyond the space occupied by the 'fish'.
Children then swap roles and repeat the game.

Shark chase!

Home

Start

Number Bonds 1

Number Bonds

Aim

To practise number bonds 2-10

Instructions

1. Copy the masters onto coloured paper/card and laminate. (N.B. One master is unmarked, so could be used for working on any total to 10).

2. Attach cord at dot (a).

Equipment needed

Coloured counters to place on the circles and number line; piece of cord.

Activities

1. Children place counters on all the circles. Children use the cord to partition the set in different ways and discuss the results, e.g. 8 is made up of 3 and 5; 3 and 5 make/equal 8. They can then record their results.

2. Place counters on the circles. Partition the set in order to answer an equation such as: $3 + \_ = 8$ or $\_ + 5 = 8$

3. Place counters on the circles. Take away a given number of counters and place on the number line. Question: "How many are left on the circles?" This could be an activity for discussion only, or results could be recorded, e.g. $8 - 5 = 3$

Alternatively, place the counters on the number line. Take away counters from the right and place on the circles.
The number left will be indicated by the position on the number line.

e.g.

●	●	●							
1	**2**	**3**	**4**	**5**	**6**	**7**	**8**	**9**	**10**

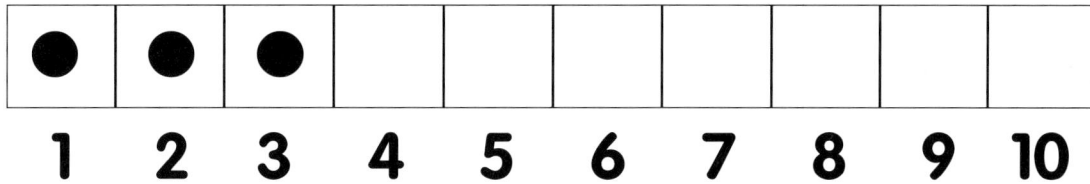

Recorded as: 8 - 5 = 3
N.B. the cord will be redundant for this activity

1	2	3	4	5	6	7	8	9	10

2

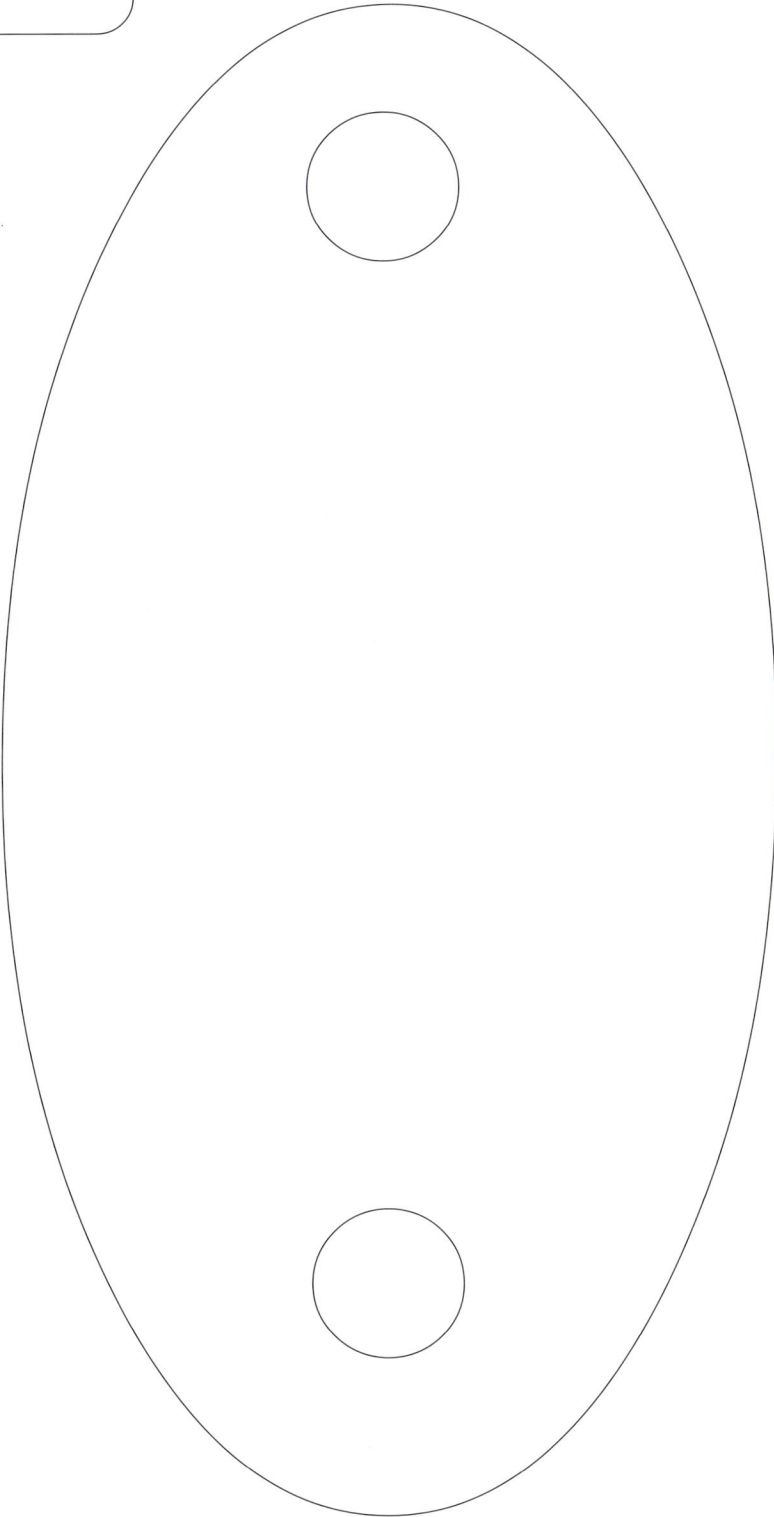

a

1 2 3 4 5 6 7 8 9 10

3

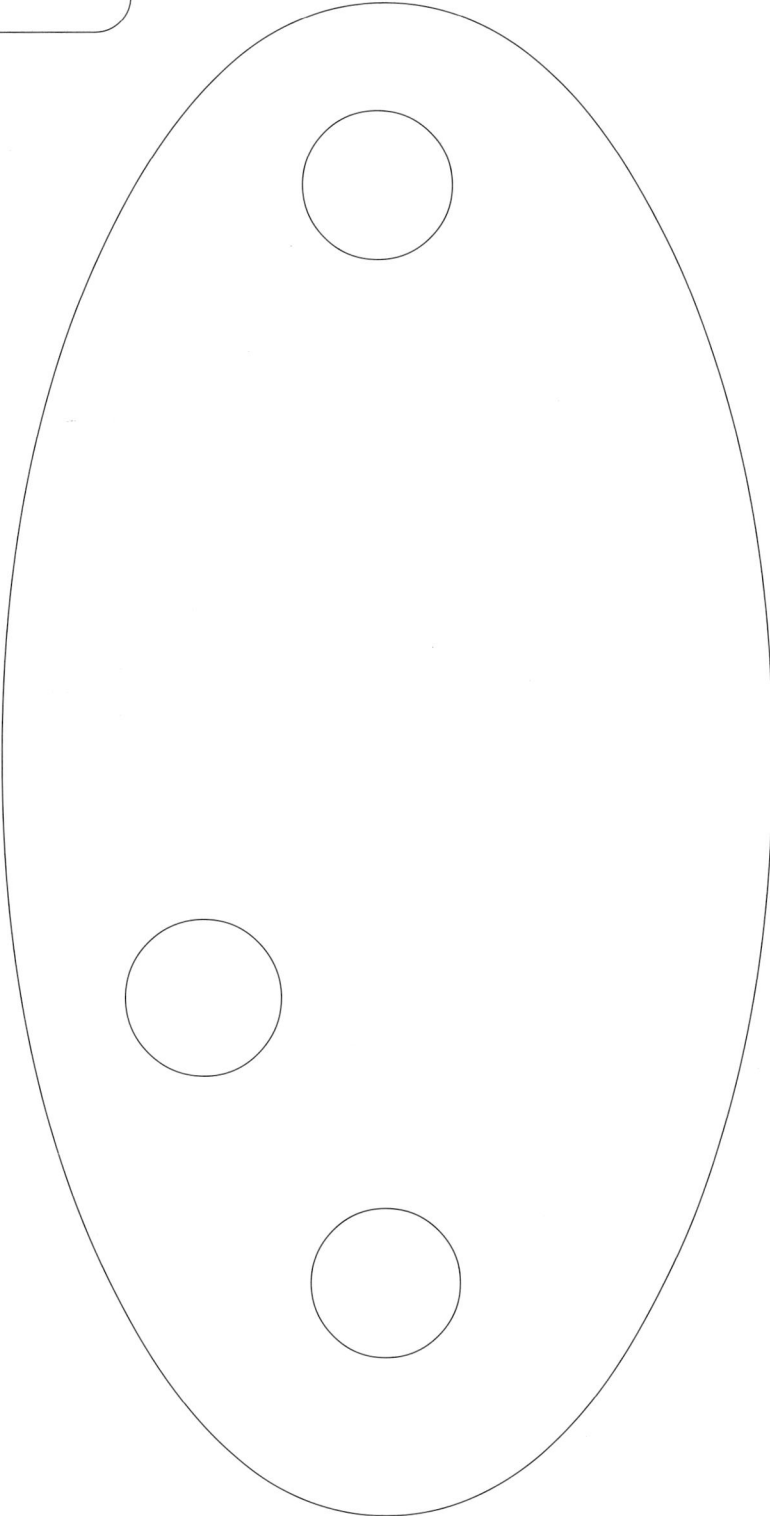

a

1 2 3 4 5 6 7 8 9 10

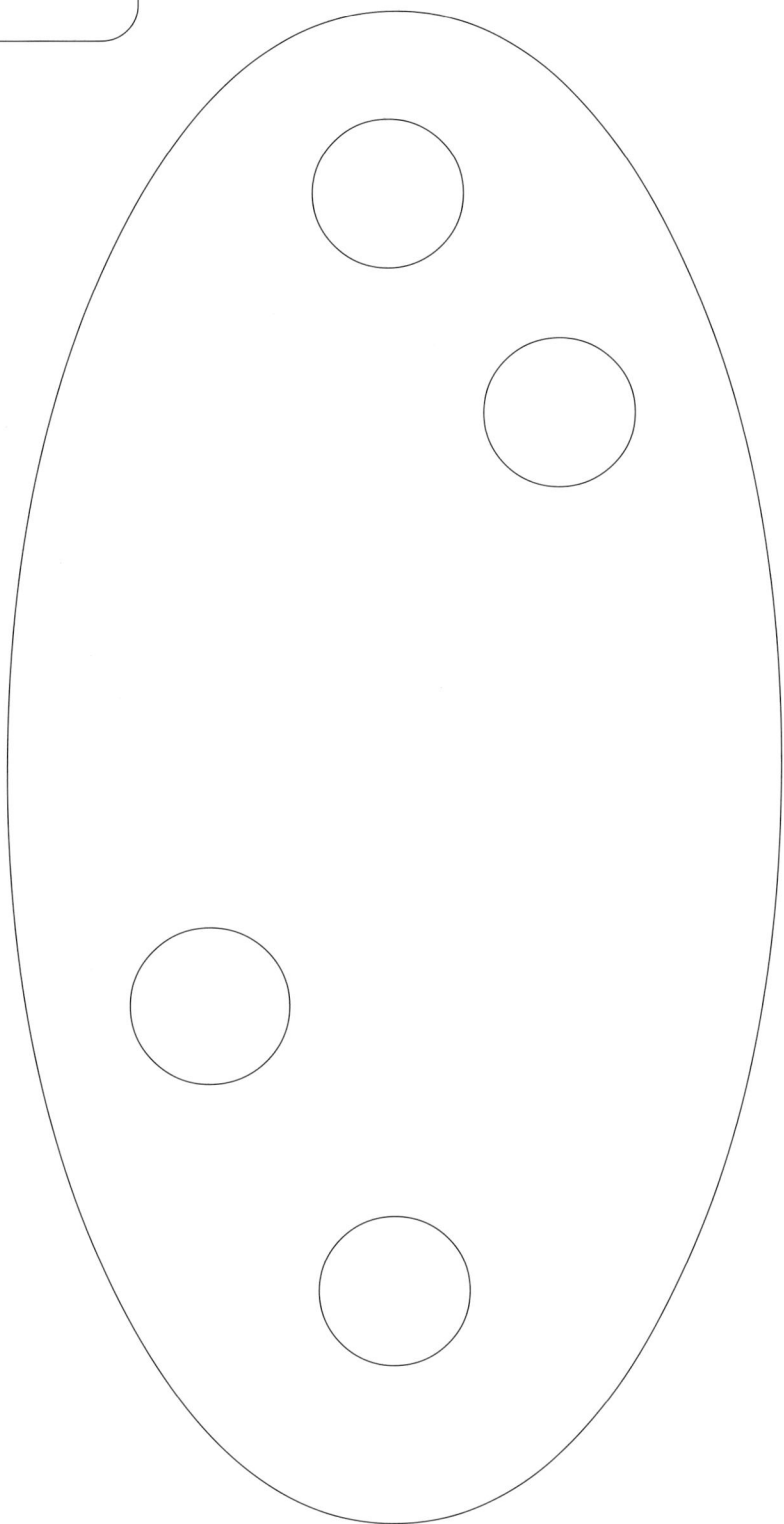

1	2	3	4	5	6	7	8	9	10

5

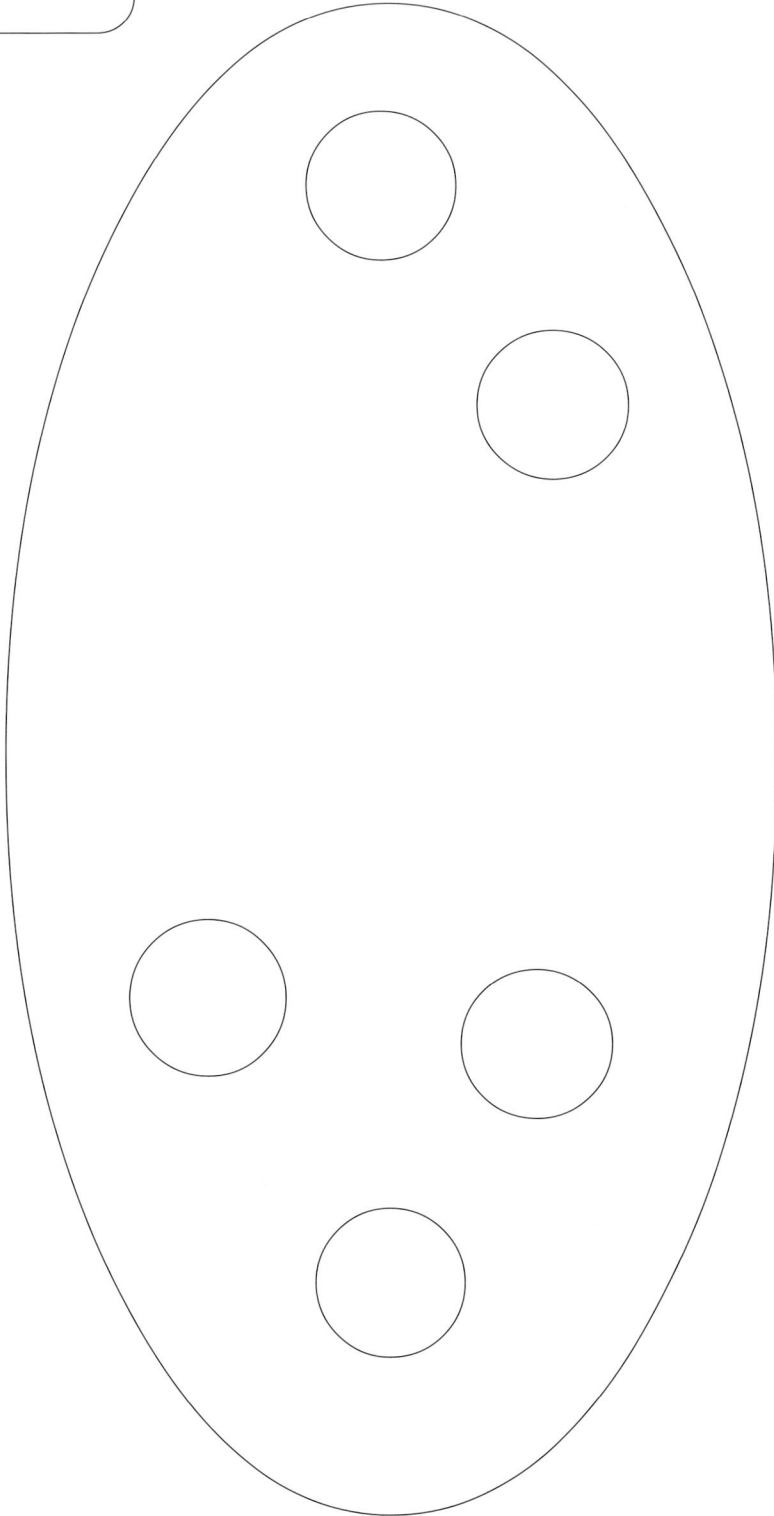

a

1 2 3 4 5 6 7 8 9 10

6

a

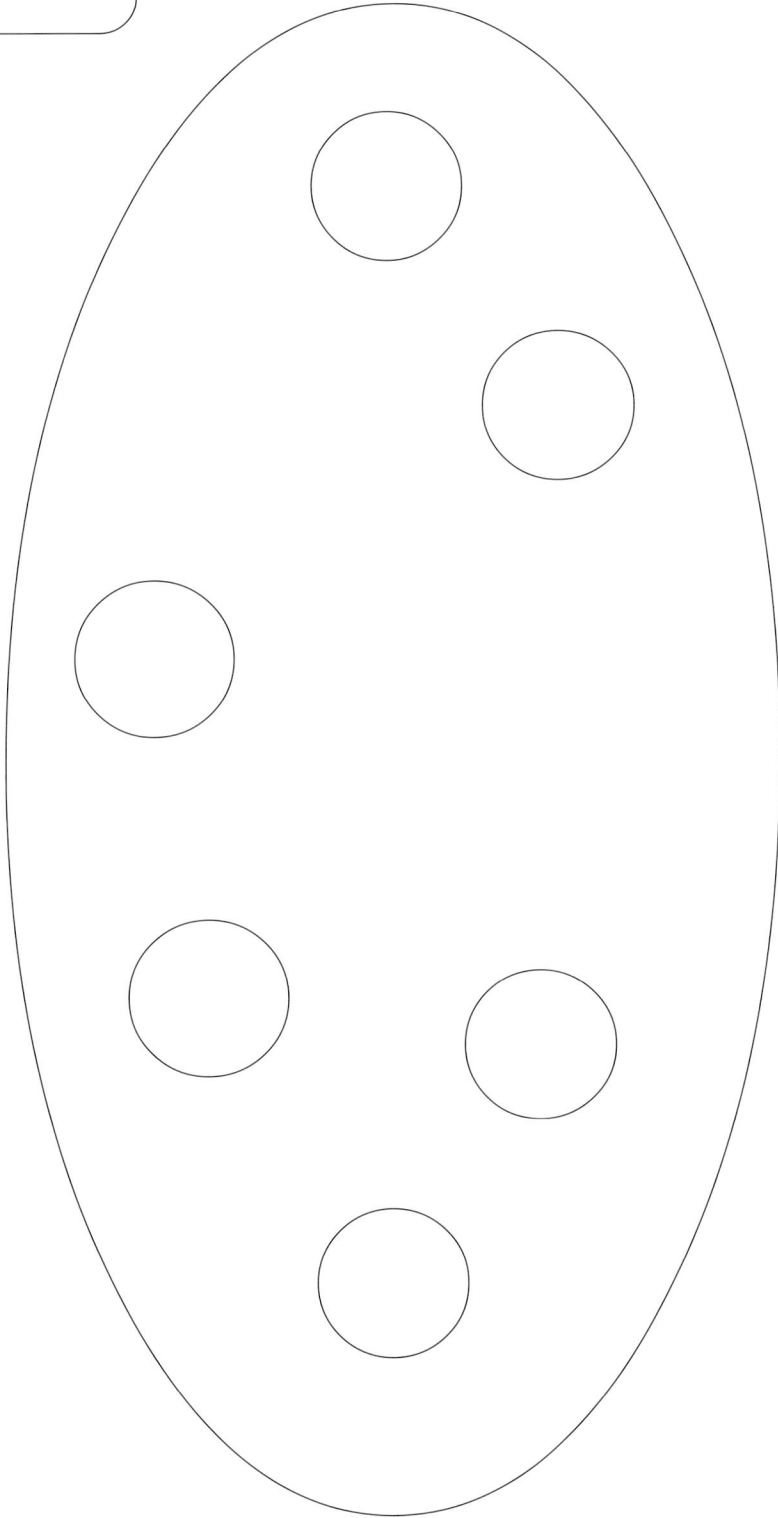

1 2 3 4 5 6 7 8 9 10

7

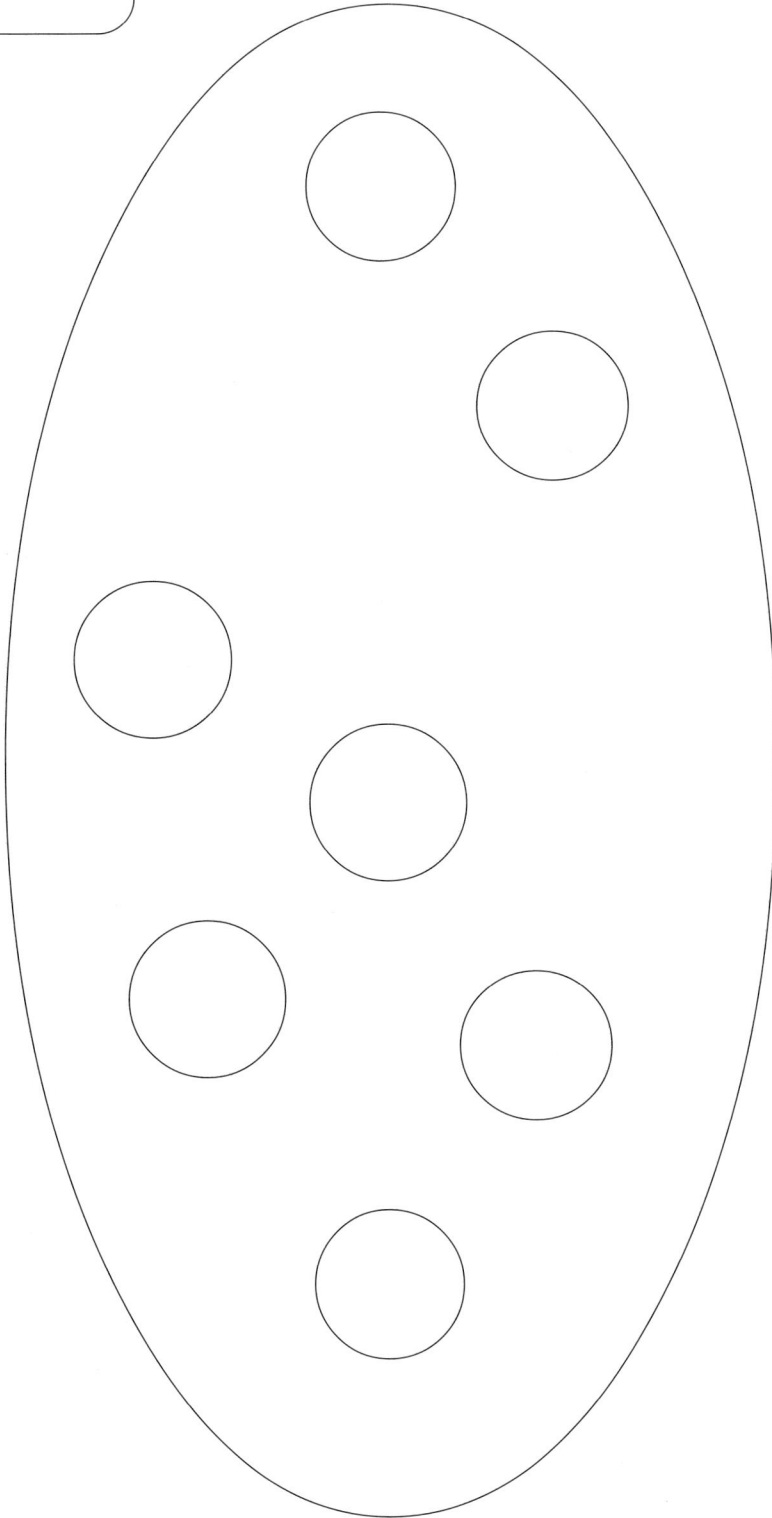

a

1 2 3 4 5 6 7 8 9 10

8

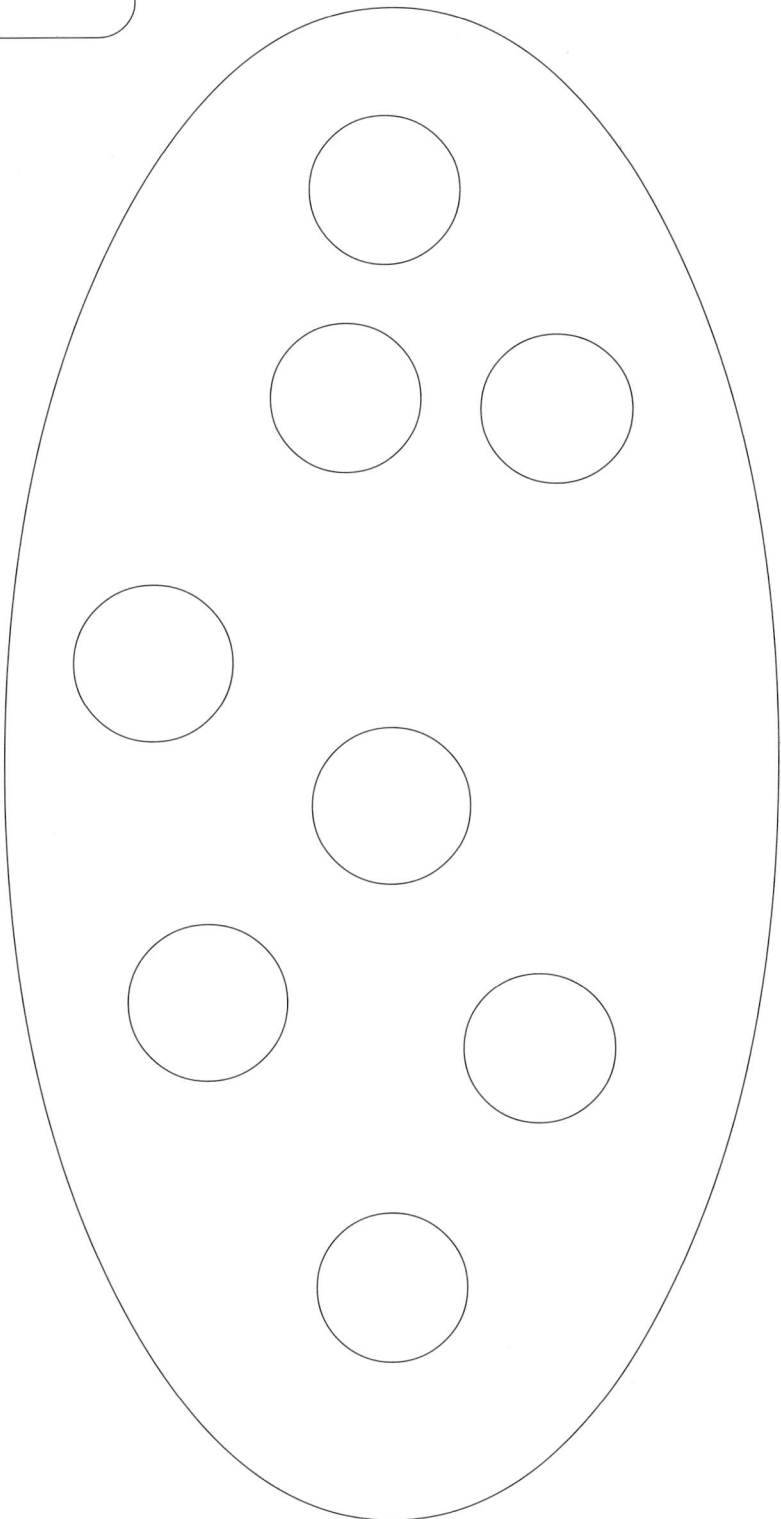

a

1 2 3 4 5 6 7 8 9 10

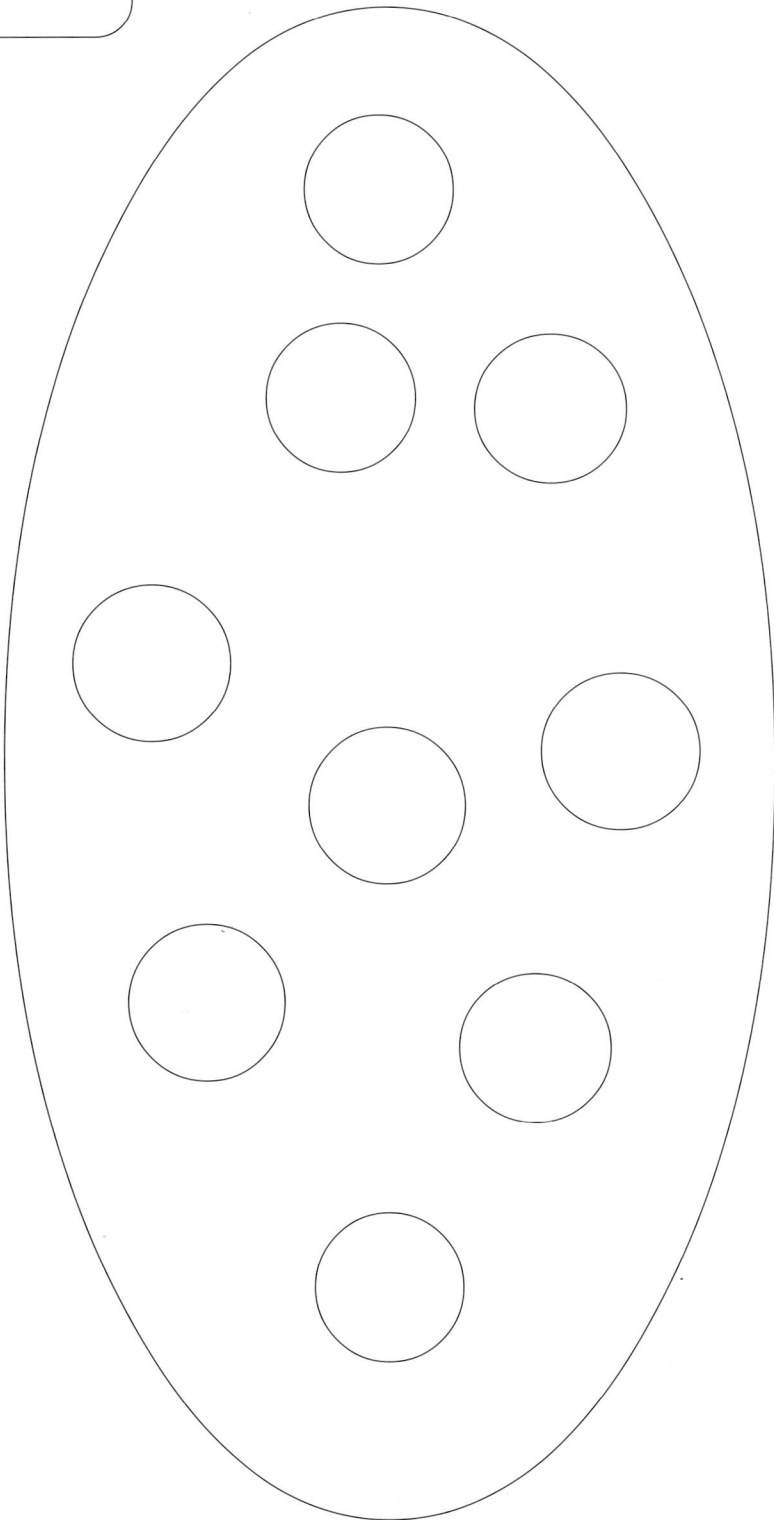

10

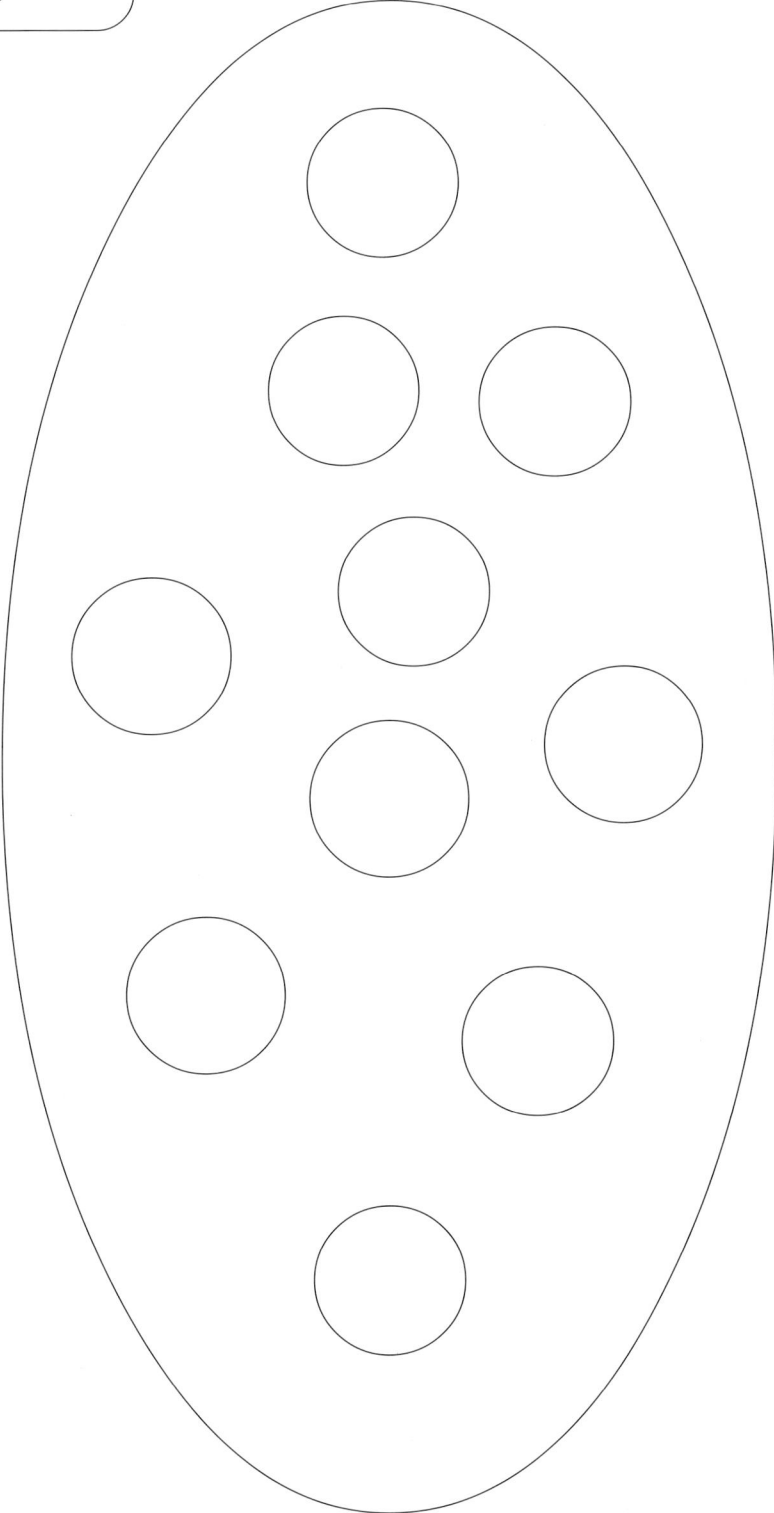

● a

1 2 3 4 5 6 7 8 9 10

Number Bonds 2

Number Bonds 2

Aim

1. To reinforce number bonds

2. To recognize relationships e.g. commutative law
(e.g. 15 x 8 = 8 x 15
        20 - 17 = 3 + 17 = 20)

Instructions

1. Copy the masters onto coloured card/paper and laminate.

2. Cut up individual numbers and symbols.

Activities

These can be used to 'record' practical/discussion work

e.g.
17 + 3 = 20	20 = 17+ 3
3 + 17 = 20	20 = 3 + 17
20 - 3 = 17	20 - 17 = 3
3 x 5 = 15	15 = 3 x 5
5 x 3 = 15	15 = 5 x 3
15 ÷ 3 = 15	15 ÷ 5 = 3

etc.

7	14	21	28
6	13	20	27
5	12	19	26
4	11	18	25
3	10	17	24
2	9	16	23
1	8	15	22

35	42	49	56
34	41	48	55
33	40	47	54
32	39	46	53
31	38	45	52
30	37	44	51
29	36	43	50

63	70	77	84
62	69	76	83
61	68	75	82
60	67	74	81
59	66	73	80
58	65	72	79
57	64	71	78

91

98

90

97

89

96

88

95

87

94

86

93

85

92

=

÷

×

+

100

99

Stepping Stones

Counting and Ordering Numbers to 20

Stepping Stones

Aim

To promote the knowledge and understanding of counting and ordering of numbers to 20. This sheet can also be used to practise Maths language: e.g. first; last; before; after; next; count on; count back; more; less; last; between.

Instructions

Photocopy and enlarge the master to A3 and laminate.

Equipment needed

Coloured counters; a die

Activities

1. Number line for addition and subtraction to 20.

2. Number recognition to 20.

3. Even and Odd numbers e.g. to be coloured by pupil.

4. Counting on and counting back.
e.g. **The Plus Minus Game.** A game for 2 players. You need a baseboard with 3 numbers coloured red and 3 coloured green at random. 2 counters and 1 die.

How to play:

Highest throw on the die starts the game.

Each pupil takes it in turn to throw the die and move their counter the indicated number of moves as shown on the die. If their counter lands on green they can move on the same number of spaces again. If their counter lands on red, they move back the same number of spaces.

The first player to land on 'FINISH' wins the game.

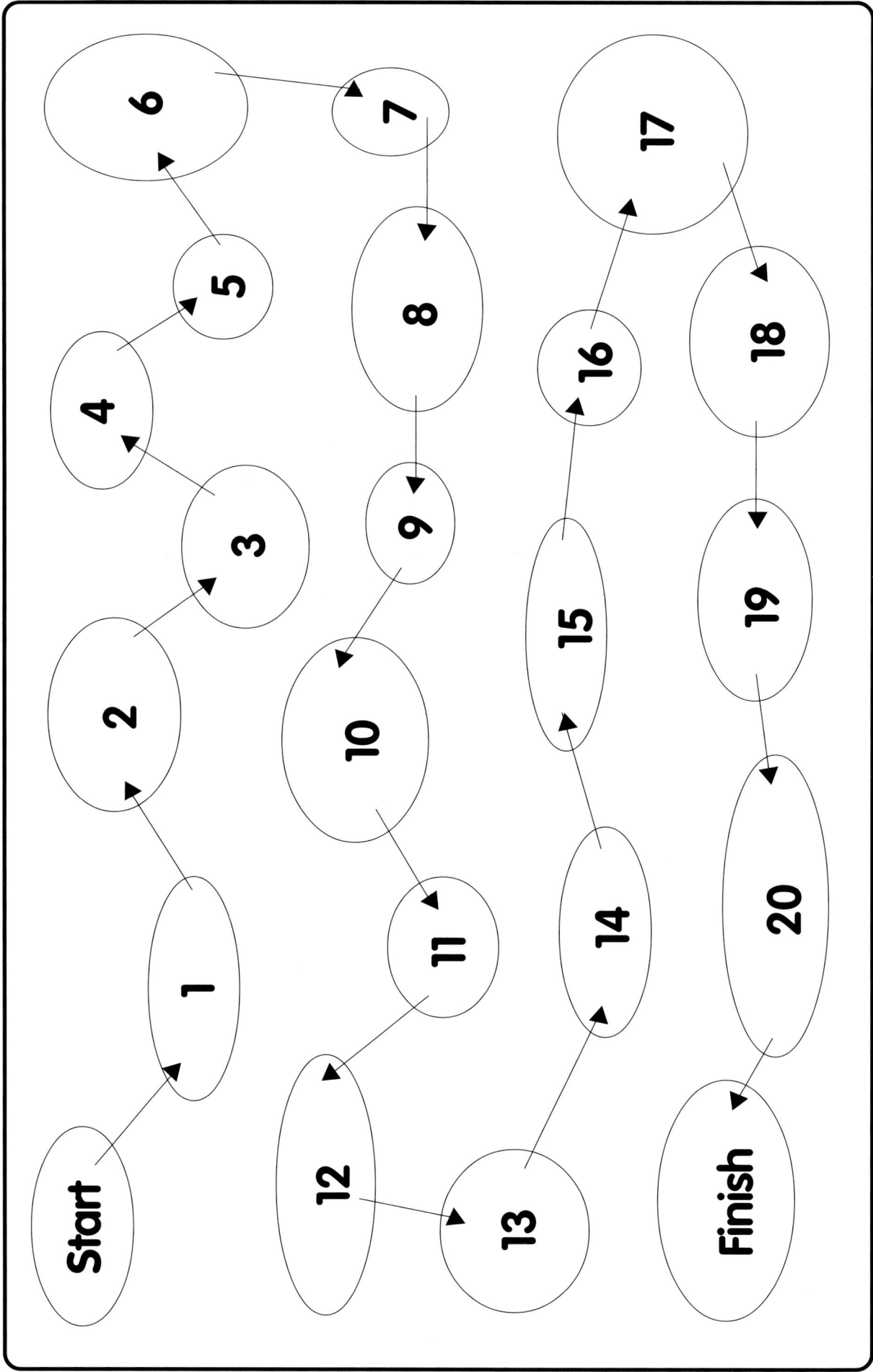

Start

1

2

3

4

5

6

7

8

9

10

11

12

13

14

15

16

17

18

19

20

Finish

Dragons
Matching by Size and Colour

Dragons

Aim

To develop matching skills and memory skills using the criteria of size and colour.

Instructions

1. Photocopy 4 copies of the master sheet.

2. Colour the Dragons so that you have 20 pairs, matching in size and colour e.g. 2 large blue dragons with yellow spots.

3. Cut out the cards.

How to Play

1. Shuffle the pack and deal all the cards among the players.

2. Players place their cards in a pile, face down in front of them.

3. In turn, the players turn up their top card and place it in the centre of the table, making a pile.

4. When a turned up card matches the card immediately beneath it on the centre pile, 'DRAGON' is called.

5. The player who calls 'DRAGON' first, takes the centre pile of cards and places them face down under his pile.
That player resumes the game by placing their next card in the centre.

6. A player who uses up all of his cards is out of the game.
The last player left in the game is the winner.

This can also be used as a Pelmanism game. It may be advisable to begin playing with a reduced number of pairs of cards.

Shape

Shape

Aim

To develop the skill of matching shapes with shape words.

Instructions

1. Photocopy shapes onto card. They will need to be copied double sided so that the shape words are on the back of the shapes.

2. Photocopy shapes and words onto separate cards.

3. Laminate.

Activities

1. With class or group, present the blank shape side and ask the children to name the shape. Discuss the number of sides, angles, size of angles, relative length of sides.
Discuss similarities, difference between shapes.

2. With class or group, present the word side of the shape.
Ask the children to identify the shape. Talk about the word.

3. For individual work, ask a child to match the shape to the word.

4. To focus on number of sides, types of angles, relative size of sides, make up a grid for the children to complete.

Name of Shape	Number of sides	Number of angles	Number of right angles

Be selective about the information given on the grid to differentiate the activity.

5. Ask the children to make shape pictures using some or all of the shapes.

6. Ask the children to identify these shapes around the school or the home. This would provide the starting point for investigations into the properties of shapes and their use in design.

square

circle

rectangle

oblong

pentagon

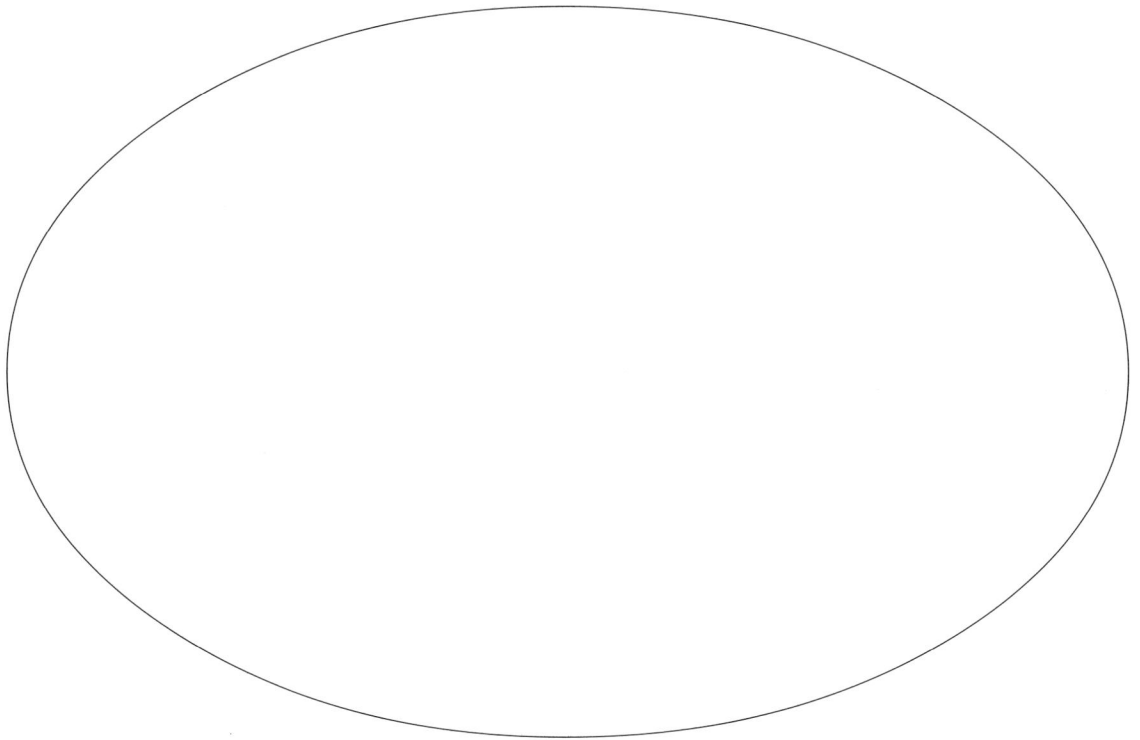

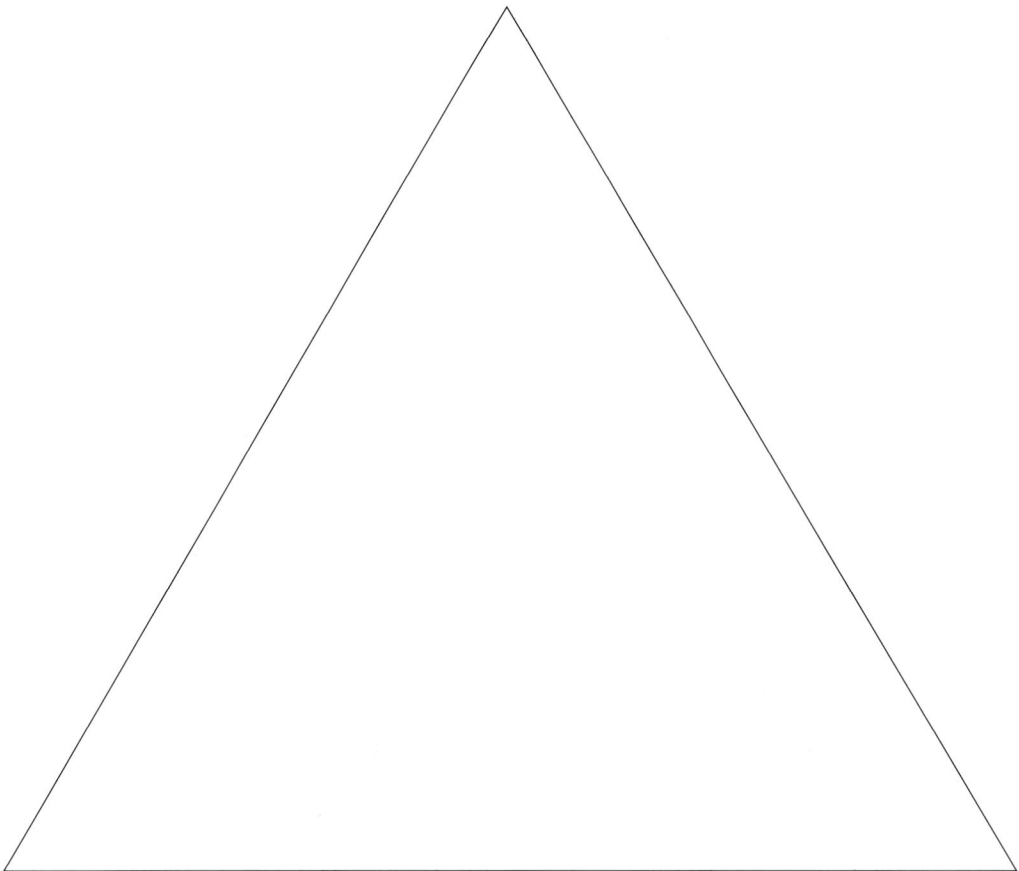

oval

triangle

hexagon

Place Value

Place Value

This consists of 5 sheets:

- Write the numeral – faces and hearts
- Write the numeral – stars and diamonds
- 2 sets of numeral cards 0-9
- Tens and units board
- Hundreds, tens and units board

Write the numeral sheets

For these two sheets an understanding that ten diamonds make a star, and ten hearts make a face is established before the sheets are used.

Tens and units board and hundreds, tens and units board

These are used to record numerals to make a number. Three dice are required. One die with hundreds on each face, one die with tens on each face, and one die with units on each face.

Up to six players can play this game together. Each player requires a hundreds, tens and units sheet and a pencil.

Players take it in turns to roll the hundred die in turn to establish who starts the game. The players then follow in value order from the highest to the lowest number thrown.

Each player rolls the hundred die again and enters the hundred number thrown onto their sheet.

Each player then rolls the tens die and enters that number onto their sheet.

The whole process is repeated with the units die.

Each player then adds up their score.

The player with the highest score wins the game.

The numeral cards can be duplicated onto card and used as an alternative to writing.

TIP! Small pieces of Blu-Tack on the back of the numeral cards will stop them moving about.

The tens and units game can be played in the same way.

Write the numeral

Write the numeral

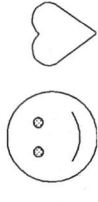

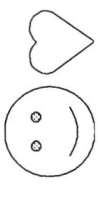

t	U
Tens	**Units**

h	t	u
Hundreds	**Tens**	**Units**

4	3	2	1	0
9	8	7	6	5
4	3	2	1	0
9	8	7	6	5

Valu-Balls

Place Value

h.t.u.

Valu-balls

Photocopy nine of the master sheets onto card.

Cut out the individual sections.

Write the numerals 100-900 on the three section pieces, the numerals 10-90 on the two section pieces and the numerals 1-9 on the single section pieces.

Laminate the sections and cut out.

Use the sections to demonstrate and develop an understanding of place value.

If the sections are enlarged they make a useful group teaching aid.

untis

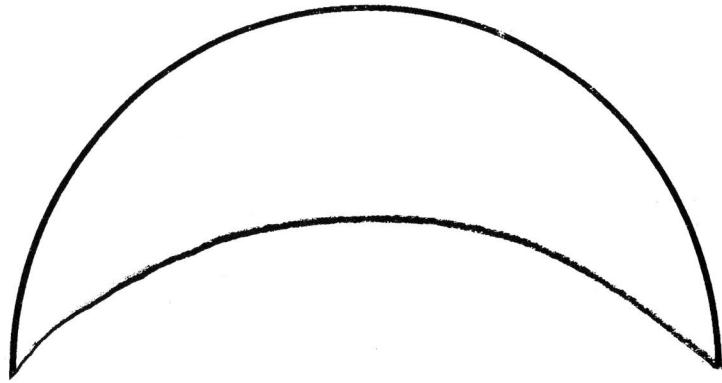

tens

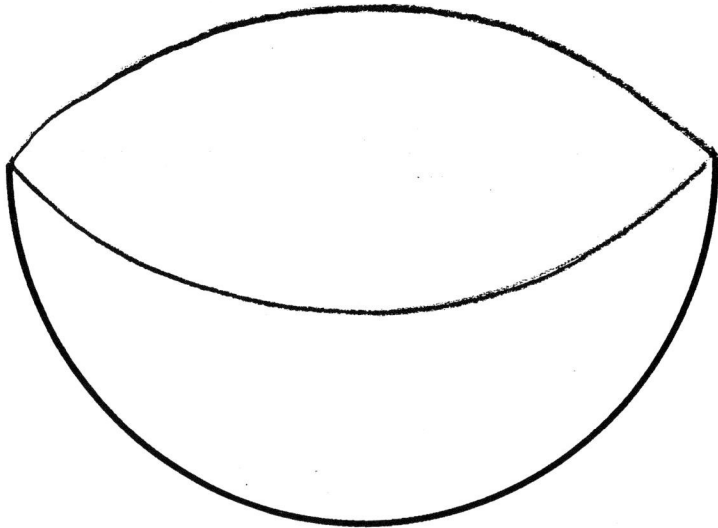

hundreds

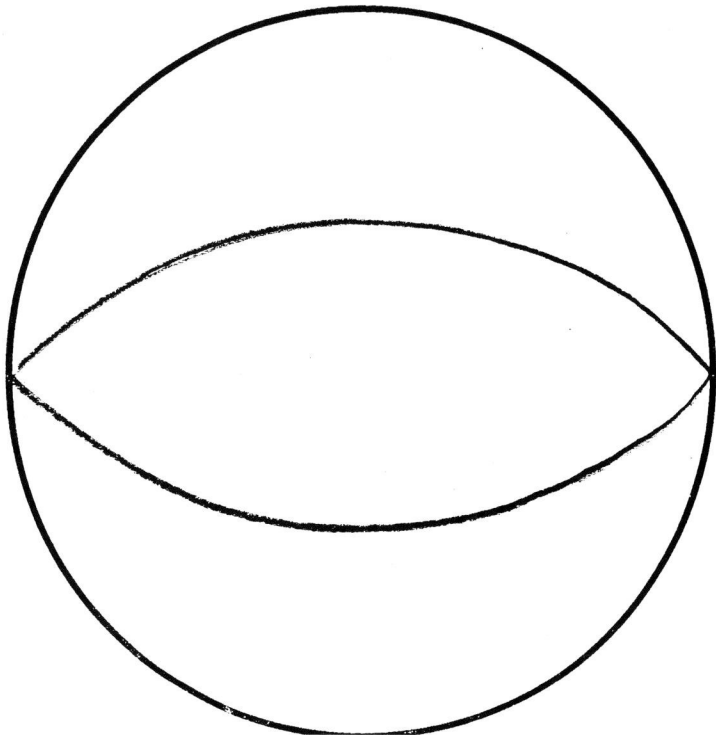

Maths Language

Maths Language

Aim

To introduce the signs and vocabulary for the four rules of number.

Contents

Vocabulary / Signs listed.
2 baseboards
● add, subtract, multiply, divide.
● add, subtract, multiply, divide, total
● answer sheet

Activities – these are progressive

1. Vocabulary / Signs – for use as:
● sight vocabulary needed for the 4 rules of number and associated activities
● sorting activities – into sets for each of the 4 rules
● display purposes.

2. Baseboards
● for matching vocabulary to the appropriate sign
● small group activities – it could help if one of the group acts as 'leader' to check responses against the answer sheet e.g. shuffle the vocabulary cards and give each pupil 4-5 cards. Put the remainder in a pile face down. Pupils take it in turns to place 1 of their cards against the correct sign on the baseboard. If they are not sure, they can exchange the card for one of the cards from the pile. Then place the unused card at the bottom of the pile. Winner is the first person to use all their cards.

3. Display – enlarge baseboard and vocabulary for display and to consolidate learning and access information for less able pupils.

+	**plus**
add	**–**
altogether	**take**
sum	**take away**
more than	**less than**
more	**difference**
count on	**difference between**

count back	times
minus	sets of
X	product
lots of	÷
groups of	share
double	divide
multiply	groups of

=

equals

total

sum of

product

is the
same as

I	•|•
+	✕

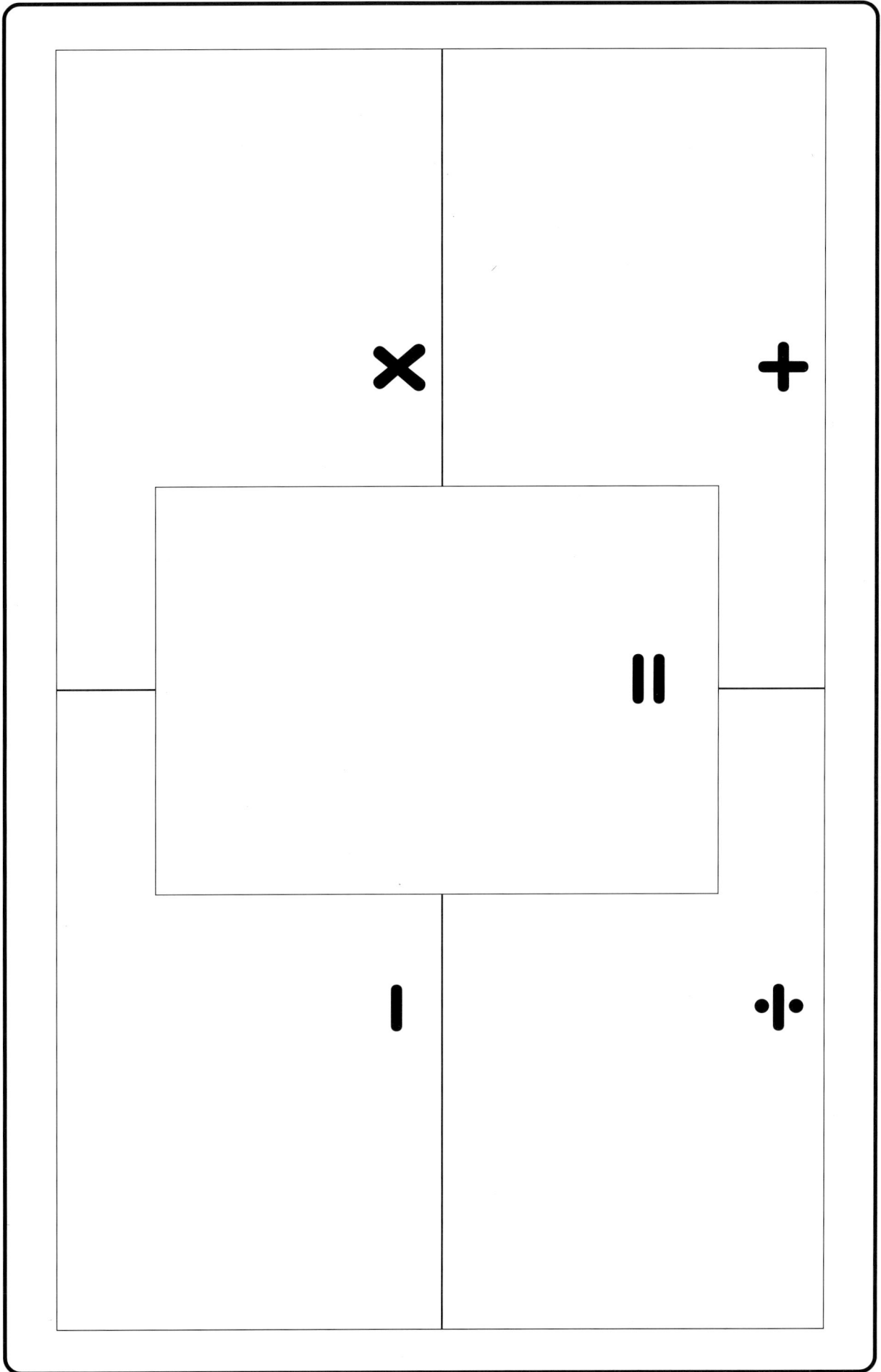

×

+

||

I

•|•

–

take   take away
less than   minus
difference
difference between
count back

÷

share
divide
groups of

=

equals   total
sum of   product
is the same as

+

add together
sum   more than
more   count on
plus

×

lots of groups of
double   multiply
times   sets of
product